Ethical
Leadership

Stephen Connock is group personnel and corporate affairs director for Eastern Group plc, a FT–SE 100 company with over £2 billion turnover, where he has responsibility for regulation, business services, HR and corporate communications. Prior to joining Eastern in 1992 he was for five years general manager (HR) at Pearl Assurance. Previously he had been employed by Philips Electronics first as group IR manager and then as group management development and training manager. He is the author of three books on HR management, including *HR Vision* (1991), an IPD publication. He has a first degree in economic history from the University of Sheffield and an M.Phil. from the London School of Economics. Well known as a conference speaker, he is also a member of the CBI National Employment Committee.

Ted Johns is an independent management consultant specialising in the improvement of organisational performance. Recent clients include Philips Electronics and SmithKline Beecham, for whom he carried out assignments in the UK, continental Europe, and the Far East on corporate value systems and ethical leadership. Prior to entering management consultancy full-time with his network, The PROSPER Consortium, he headed the personnel management division at the Thames Valley Business School and directed the School's M.Sc. in personnel management. He has written several books (on customer care, time management, and organisational change) and was for 11 years managing editor of the *Sundridge Park Management Review*. He is an examiner for the IPD, the Institute of Chartered Secretaries and Administrators, and the Chartered Institute of Marketing. With a Ph.D. in organisational behaviour, an MA in sociology, and a first degree in economics, he is a chartered secretary, a Fellow of the IPD, and a full corporate member of the Institute of Management Consultants.

The Institute of Personnel and Development is the leading publisher of books and reports for personnel and training professionals and students and for all those concerned with the effective management and development of people at work. For full details of all our titles please telephone the Publishing Department on 0181 263 3387.

Ethical
Leadership

Stephen Connock
and
Ted Johns

**INSTITUTE OF PERSONNEL
AND DEVELOPMENT**

Typeset by Photoprint, Torquay
Printed in Great Britain by
The Cromwell Press, Wiltshire

British Library Cataloguing in Publication Data
A catalogue record for this book is available from the British Library

ISBN 0–85292–561–1

The views expressed in this book are the authors' own, and may not necessarily reflect those of the IPD.

IPD House, Camp Road, London SW19 4UX
Tel.: 0181 971 900 Fax: 0181 263 3333
Registered charity no. 1038333. A company limited by guarantee.
Registered in England no. 2931892.
Registered office as above.

Contents

Acknowledgements

It is customary to say, and we say it with particular conviction, that many managers, staff, academics and consultants have helped shape our book. Some did so without realising it, since we discussed our embryonic views about ethical leadership with them before it had occurred to us to write at length on the subject.

Among the individuals who co-operated with us more directly, we recognise with gratitude the contributions made by:

- Alison Train and Chris Gray of Eastern Group – for helpful comments on an early draft of some of the chapters;
- Geoff Ribbens of The PROSPER Consortium – for continually stressing the need to differentiate between 'ethics', 'values' and 'morality';
- Bernard Cooke, Management Development Manager for Nuffield Hospitals – for being cynical about the whole concept, and therefore being visualised as a typical reader; and
- Matthew Reisz, Commissioning Editor at the IPD – for tolerating our constant failure to meet deadlines.

Neither of the authors would have produced anything without the support of people close to us. For Steve, this means Margaret, Adrian and Mark; for Ted, it means his partner, Wendy. Seeing their names in print is feeble compensation for the sacrifices they have made in allowing us the time and space to write – but it will have to do until the royalties come flooding in.

Preface

Let us first issue some disclaimers. *Ethical Leadership* is not an abstract text on business ethics. The market is already saturated with such books. It is intended to be a practical and pragmatic contribution to the advancement of best practice in corporate behaviour. In essence, what we seek to do is to discuss and explain:

- *what* we mean by ethical leadership
- *why* managers and organisations should practice ethical leadership
- *how* ethical leadership can become a reality.

Although not principally academic, our approach is nonetheless rigorous, based on a conceptual framework that combines both macro-ethical and micro-ethical dimensions.

We believe that ethical leadership is a potential source of competitive advantage. However, our arguments for adopting ethical leadership in organisations do not rely on that possibility. Our stance instead reflects increasing concern about corporate and individual ethics among all stakeholders with investments in organisational effectiveness – the shareholders, employees, suppliers, customers, and the public at large. Ethical leadership, if properly pursued, enables employee actions to be aligned more closely to their ethical aspirations; it creates confidence among customers; it improves relationships with external agencies (especially where regulation and compliance are involved); it generates synergy with suppliers; it benefits the bottom line. At the same time there are higher-order reasons for demonstrating ethical leadership which go beyond the purely materialistic and instrumental. Indeed, if our reasons were straightforwardly materialistic, then the case for ethical leadership would itself be unethical, because it would rest on the proposition that being ethical is merely a means to an end, rather than an end in itself.

Of course, we are not so foolish as to deny the instrumental benefits. If we are ethical, we may encourage reciprocal behaviour of the same kind; we may attract ethically minded recruits; we are likely to find more customers and retain them for longer. That these are corporate advantages nobody can deny, yet we cannot emphasise too strongly that our advocacy for ethical leadership is founded on arguments of principle rather than calculations of expediency.

Our motive in writing this book stems partly from personal commitment to its theme but also from our experience in promoting ethical leadership as senior HR practitioners and as consultants. The book is derived from our combined observations and ideas. It contains no detailed case-studies but supplies an overview of benchmark standards for ethical leadership illuminated by many examples from organisations which have already found ethical leadership to be a worthwhile exercise.

The book is not prescriptive. At various points we say that organisations must think through for themselves the implications of the points we are making. Such thinking-through is essential, no matter how painful it may be. Given the variety of corporate scenarios to which the concepts of ethical leadership may be applied, it would have been danger-ous to have produced a single, prefabricated, ready-to-eat recipe.

Yet we remain firmly action-centred. We want things to happen as a result of what we have assembled here. We genuinely believe (without patronising our readers) that many organisations could benefit from an explicit ethical leadership programme. It follows logically from a focus on total quality management and customer care; it is entirely consistent with the values of the post-industrial climate in which we function at present. Ethical leadership is an idea whose time has come.

Stephen Connock
Ted Johns
October, 1995

1

Introduction: The Importance of Business Ethics

As we write, ethical issues abound. The speaker of the House of Commons describes the action of one MP who puts down an amendment to a bill in the name of another MP as 'distasteful'.[1] The Southampton goalkeeper, Bruce Grobbelaar, is accused of match-fixing. The wife of the chairman of the National Grid Company hits the tabloid headlines for having shares transferred to her for legitimate tax-efficiency reasons. She touches a raw nerve – that of 'fat cat' remuneration – and in so doing raises the deep and complex issue of 'distributive justice'.[2] Anita Roddick, co-founder of the Body Shop, joins a street protest against Shell's operation in Nigeria, but in turn has her ethics questioned by the American magazine *Business Ethics*.[3] A MORI survey reported in the *Sunday Times* in June 1995 says that two-thirds of Britain's leading companies have been victims of serious fraud by employees, the survey identifying 'greed' as a central motive.[4]

Just as ethics becomes the focus of attention, so alternative views suggest a more cynical perspective. As a *Daily Telegraph* feature writer on 2 September 1994 put it:

> I am worried by the notion of a boom in ethics. I expect it to lead to compliance procedures and committee work and the ticking off of points on codes and check-lists. This is no substitute for good conduct, any more than the Cadbury Code of Company Directors is a substitute for good direction.

This viewpoint is echoed by companies. For example, C & J Clark state:

> Like many things, ethics is something that a company of 160 years' standing has built into its systems rather than

1

something specific. I think we should shrink away from an
ethics policy as it implies you need one![5]

These are genuine concerns. Ethics is not just about having a
values statement, or a published code of practice. These are
helpful because they indicate a policy direction. What matters
most is ethical behaviour at all levels, and this requires ethical
leadership.

What is ethical leadership?

Despite large numbers of obscure definitions of ethics, our
view is relatively straightforward. Ethics is about fairness,
about deciding what is right or wrong, about defining the
practices and rules which underpin responsible conduct
between individuals and groups.

We recognise that the words and phrases used in such a
definition are capable of considerable interpretation, about
which whole books could be – and are – written. Our purpose
in this book, however, is to provide a more pragmatic
approach to the study of ethics within business. Ethical issues
in business impact upon everyone. As Elaine Sternberg put it:

> The key business ethics concern is the way that the
> business conducts itself in its ordinary, everyday routine
> activities. The way the firm deals with its staff and its
> customers, the way it designs and supports its products,
> the way it awards contracts and apportions blame . . .
> these are the key determinants of whether a business is
> ethical . . .[6]

Ordinary decency and fairness are vital components of
ethics. What then of ethical *leadership*? Our emphasis on
leadership raises the issue of clarity of vision, and long-term
consistency in pursuing this vision, and of an integrated ethical
dimension to the vision. As Tom Peters put it in *Thriving on
Chaos*, leadership involves the highest integrity and

visions which are clear – and lived with almost frightening consistency, in small as well as in large ways.[7]

In a context of rapid organisational and product change, a company's vision and accompanying values can be vital elements to provide a sense of direction and predictability, setting the pattern and tone for the organisation. Ethical judgements – choices about resource allocation, about benefits to customers or to shareholders, about self-interest versus the interests of others – can be facilitated if ethical considerations have been embraced in the development of the vision and values.

Laura Nash, in her definition of business ethics, said

> Business ethics is the study of how personal moral norms apply to the activities and goals of commercial enterprise. It is not a separate moral standard, but the study of how the business context poses its own unique problems for the moral person who acts as an agent of this system.[8]

We agree that business ethics is not a separate moral standard but one that is thoroughly integrated within answers to deep questions about the business:

- why does it exist?
- what is its purpose?

These same questions have preoccupied philosophers for centuries, albeit in relation to the individual:

- why do I exist?
- what is my purpose?

For the company, the answers should lie in the vision and this will be inseparable from ethical considerations. Here we agree with Freeman and Gilbert:

> strategy and ethics go hand in hand. Strategy is concerned with purposes and values, and so is ethics. Concepts and

models of strategy are necessarily built on some views of
ethics, and we will do better to be explicit about the
flavour of ethics we want to defend.[9]

Being explicit about ethics and corporate values is a relatively
novel experience for European managers in particular. That
makes Jan Carlsson's contribution all the more conspicuous. A
key player in the change of fortunes at SAS, he said in 1988:
'Allowing an individual to share your vision gives that person
greater understanding and motivation. That, to me, is strategic
leadership'.[10]

Theories of ethics

Theories of ethics may appear remote and unimportant to most
managers, but underlying many business considerations are
different philosophical approaches to ethical issues. A brief
review of three approaches may be helpful. The three approaches
discussed here are:

- Social ethics
- Transcendental ethics
- Tactical ethics

We consider each in turn.

Social ethics

The word 'ethics' is derived from the Greek *ēthikos and ēthos*
and, according to the *Shorter Oxford English Dictionary*,
means the 'prevalent tone or sentiment of a people or
community'. For the Greeks, ethics was a practical science
because the basic rules for civilised living were founded on the
consensus recognition of what was generally accepted in
society as 'good'. It was the ethos, or climate of opinion in a

society, which determined the standards by which right or wrong conduct was to be judged. Because this kind of ethics was determined directly by the society to which the individual belonged, the term 'social ethics' is an apt description.

Greek 'society' was the city-state, and the city-state's ethos was set by the Greek citizens (in the days before political correctness, slaves played no significant part in the process of defining the behavioural norms). In each city-state the standards of ethics were determined by a relatively small number of people, therefore, but the common thread – indeed, the prime incentive for ethical conduct – was the need for social acceptability.

Different city-states had different ethical climates, and ethical standards were generally lower in relations between people of different cities than between fellow citizens of the same city. In this model, while a society may have high ethical standards within itself, social ethics can often mean that a citizen can act outside that society, in its best interests, without any sense of right or wrong about what he is doing.

The weakness of social ethics is that it breaks down in situations involving relationships between differing societies (or 'stakeholders' in business terms). An extension of this point is Marx's observation that social ethics is based only on accepted standards within a specific social class (eg, the citizens in the Greek city-state). Anyone outside this privileged circle need feel no commitment to the proclaimed ethical standards.

The strengths of social ethics include the fact that the ethical standards themselves are relatively easy to define. Moreover, it is much easier to be identified with the interests of one's own society than with a set of abstract ethical principles. If social ethics reflects loyalty to the city-state – or, in modern terms, to one's family, one's party, one's country or one's organisation – then it can be an easy, convenient substitute for any other conceivable set of ethical standards in relationships outside the primary group. Indeed, social ethics in general is little more than a sophisticated version of group loyalty, and to that extent

many corporate vision statements and codes of values rely on
the logic of the assumptions surrounding social ethics.

Transcendental ethics

This framework relies on absolute concepts of right and wrong,
on universal standards of fairness, rightness and justice which
should be applied equally in all human societies (and, by
inference, all business organisations).

Transcendental ethics has its origins in two linked causal
factors:

- The growing realisation that social ethics does not cater
  adequately for relationships between different societies.
- The desire to show that the ethical standards in one's own
  society are superior to all others; this can be done by
  claiming universal applicability.

Most world religions possess a transcendental ethos, giving
rise to standards of right conduct to be observed without any
social, cultural or geographical restriction. Similarly, there are
several non-religious philosophies – political, humanitarian or
materialistic – which give rise to transcendental ethics.

Some commercial organisations seek to operate their value-
systems in a transcendental manner. SmithKline Beecham's
five core values and nine leadership practices are intended for
worldwide adoption without any regard to cultural differences;
Cargill Incorporated, the global commodity company, seeks to
comply with its own ethical principles in every country where it
does business; Novell practises its Mormon guidelines everywhere.

Tactical ethics

Many people observe ethical standards in their conduct, not
because they have any great love for, or loyalty to their own

societies or principles, but because it suits them – whether in their private lives, professional capacities, or business activities. Thus, law-abiding people may observe the ethical standards embodied in legal frameworks not out of any conviction that the law is right, but simply to avoid the penalties arising from infringement. Some individuals will practise social ethics because they see it as a means of securing social advancement for themselves, rather than because they have genuinely internalised the moral precepts involved.

In these and similar instances, ethics are practised out of convenience and the pursuit of ulterior motives, most commonly the enhancement or optimisation of self-interest. Ethical behaviour in this category is different from social ethics and transcendental ethics because it is based not on right or wrong but on other considerations – commonly, what is advantageous for the individual. Ironically, then, the individual's actual motives may be less worthy than the ethical standards apparently being applied.

Much of the current practice of business ethics is of a tactical nature. Employees will obey codes of conduct established by their organisations when they see that compliance will best further their own advancement, or non-compliance will be penalised. Moreover, firms themselves behave tactically: reasonably enough, they want a reputation for being 'ethical' if such a reputation attracts customers.

These three approaches to ethics will be identified at various points in this book. In Chapter 2, for example, we will review within a business context the objectives of different stakeholders – especially shareholders, customers, and employees – in a way which limits the usefulness of social ethics. We do not see a 'privileged circle' setting the ethical principles underpinning right or wrong. We have reservations, too, about transcendental ethics, because there will be different ethical considerations in different parts of the world. We know, for example, that attitudes towards hospitality are very different in Japan compared to the UK. As to tactical ethics, we recognise the day-to-day realities enshrined in this theory. It is always likely to be hard – but not impossible – to bring business people to a point where they can see actions as intrinsically good in themselves. This being so, ethical behaviour based on what is advantageous for the individual is understandable.

At this point we believe it helps (drawing on Aristotle) to see ethics as a means to an end – the end being the declared purpose (vision) of the organisation. Ethical principles and behaviour are those which most contribute to achieving the organisation's purpose. These ethical values can be defined alongside the vision. In so doing, managers and staff are provided with some ethical direction. We subdivide this ethical direction into macro-ethics and micro-ethics, and consider these issues in detail in Chapters 3 and 4.

Why should leaders act ethically?

It is our view that in today's commercial climate there can be competitive advantage in adopting an explicitly ethical profile. This was one of the principal sources of the reputation now enjoyed by Marks & Spencer.

John Collins, reviewing business problems in the USA looked at the issue of ethical leadership from a more defensive viewpoint as well:

> It is in a company's self-interest to be ethical not only because it is more likely to be successful, but also because it can avoid being much worse off.[11]

He then quotes company examples, such as Exxon and their oil spillage catastrophe, to demonstrate that those companies would want their employees to choose to follow the ethical course if they could do things all over again.

> Thus, good ethics is like a good insurance policy. It may not get us anything, but it sure can prevent us from losing a lot.[12]

Within the UK, a company such as British Airways, still tainted by the 'dirty tricks' revealed by Virgin in a number of high-profile law-suits, may support this viewpoint. Empowerment strategies, linked to delayering and downsizing, mean that individual decisions are more likely to have far-reaching consequences for the organisation overall. The command-and-control style of management had more built-in safeguards to protect the organisation's reputation. Businesses adopting empowerment strategies should be the first to embrace ethical leadership, thereby providing managers and staff with a clear understanding of the organisation's vision and ethical values. Our reference in the last paragraph to the organisation's reputation needs further underlining. Ethics books and articles often try to persuade us of the important link between ethics and the bottom line.[13] However, the impact on the company's reputational assets may be more far-reaching than can be quantified in terms of short-term turnover or profitability. As a writer in the *Observer* on 24 April 1994 put it:

> What . . . management lapses have in common is the incalculable damage inflicted on each organisation's most important asset – its reputation.

Higher standards are also being used to judge corporate actions, whether in the field of customer service, pollution control, or equal opportunities. Reputations can be at risk from difficulties beyond traditional areas such as safety or product quality, although these remain important. Indeed, one aspect of the shifting role of corporate leaders is the movement of business executives into the role of explicit 'social managers'. This shift is occurring partly because of customers' choosing products from a different perspective. As Stephen King puts it:

> That is, consumers' choice will depend less on an evaluation of the functional benefits to them of a product or

service, more on an assessment of the people behind it – their skills, attitudes, integrity, behaviour, styles, responsiveness, greenism, language: the whole company culture, in fact.[14]

He goes on:

There are some broader implications from the move to company brands. For instance, if the staff become the crucial brand-builders and communicators, there may have to be some changes in staff policies . . . Companies may have to give more attention to clarifying strategies; to the role of the personnel director in marketing; to training, motivation and leadership; to identifying and establishing a corporate culture.[15]

We return in Chapter 8 to the key role of HR in this area.

Changing social pressures, then, both from inside and outside the organisation have influenced the priorities of top executives. As we have said already, the pressures from inside include empowered, independent-minded employees; the pressures from outside originate from highly-organised pressure groups, well-informed shareholders and institutional investors, environmental lobbies, and so forth. The result is that senior management are forced to pay attention to issues apparently unrelated to business practice as traditionally defined, such as the social costs of buy-outs and relocations, education and health care, or long-term/short-term ecological problems. It is widely believed (whether accurately or not) that the 'success' of business in meeting consumer desires has automatically led to a degradation of both global and local ecosystems, and that this degradation is accelerating its pace.

Ethical leadership is more important than ever

Alongside those external trends, the radical pace of organisational change in the private and public sectors alike has also created considerable difficulties within organisations. Many staff have the feeling there have been too many changes, and sometimes feel those have been badly managed. Long-service staff feel particularly undervalued as newcomers criticise the 'old' practices and values. A perceived obsession with cost-cutting adds to the problems, and at any point in time there will be staff waiting to leave under a voluntary severance or retirement scheme.

Overstretched resources and job insecurity can lead to a lack of teamwork and ownership of problems. People may feel issues have not been thought through. Headquarters staff blame business-unit staff, and vice versa. There may be a feeling that a siege mentality exists in the organisation.

Do you recognise any of this? If so, ethical leadership will be necessary. In the process of responding to these problems, the following mistakes should be avoided:

- insensitivity to the manner in which change impacts upon the psychological contract of the employees
- failure to periodically diagnose the current psychological contract with various groups of employees, the result being that management is out of touch with what these groups expect to offer or receive from the organisation
- failure adequately to communicate and explain the change to the employees, so that they draw inaccurate and misleading conclusions about the implications of change for their psychological contract.

In addition to keeping the goals of change firmly in mind, and avoiding the typical errors associated with change management, there are several positive steps needed to motivate for change, manage the transition, and shape the political dynamics of change. Warren Bennis and Burt Nanus argue that one of the most important roles for a leader is to grab the attention of the organisation by creating a vision of the future which can act as a motivating purpose. A clear purpose is used by effective leaders to energise the organisation. As these authors put it:

When the organisation has a clear sense of purpose,
direction and desired future state and when this image is
widely shared, individuals are able to find their own roles
both in the organisation and in the larger society . . . This
empowers individuals and confers status upon them
because they see themselves as part of a worthwhile
enterprise. They gain a sense of importance, as they are
transformed . . . to human beings engaged in a creative
and purposeful venture.[16]

These authors also see that values act to bind the emotions
of employees to the organisation – and values are inexorably
linked to ethical leadership.

These points will be discussed in greater depth in later
chapters, and include recognising the perceptions of management and staff (Chapter 2), developing a vision with ethical
principles in mind (Chapter 3), providing guidelines to help
employees define appropriate ethical behaviour (Chapter 4)
and developing ethical values (Chapter 5).

An overview

In this book we aim to be practical, but within a conceptual
framework. We dislike too much jargon – and most textbooks
on ethics are unreadable. Few provide company examples to
illustrate points. We have tried to keep the subject-matter
straightforward and give examples of organisational practice.

The following analysis provides a brief overview:

Chapter 2 covers *ethical issues in business*. Managers face
rising pressures on costs, and on maintaining profit
margins. Surveys show that ethics does not have a high
priority. The pressures on managers to behave unethically
are reviewed, including job insecurity, performance-
related pay, and personal ambition. The ethical obligation
to different stakeholders – shareholders, customers, staff,
suppliers and the community – is then discussed. Finally,

two overriding ethical issues are examined: ethics in different cultures and ethics and negotiating skills.

Chapter 3 analyses *macro-ethics – balancing priorities.* Here we review the objectives of different stakeholders, drawing out areas of conflict. Stakeholder theory is then subject to some criticism – who are the stakeholders? Should they be given additional rights? Alternative theories are reviewed, including the 'no harm' principle and the 'principle of engagement'. We advance our own method of reconciling priorities through the development of a coherent and long-term vision. This vision is analysed by type – shareholder value, customer value, multi-stakeholders, market position, and aspirational. We then examine the association between developing a vision and embracing ethical principles.

Chapter 4 – micro-ethics, the practical agenda – examines how an organisation can identify and develop procedures to handle those ethical issues which managers and staff tackle from day to day. This includes interview pro-grammes and ethical audit questionnaires. The form, content, style, advantages and disadvantages of codes of business conduct are considered. Finally the ethical agenda is explored, with a concentration on gifts and hospitality, personal conflicts of interest, confidentiality, and relations with suppliers. Examples of company codes are quoted as illustrations of best practice.

Chapter 5 examines *tackling ethics through values.* We see values as having both prescriptive and proscriptive ele-ments. Ten factors are identified to support the import-ance of ethical values. The link between vision and values is identified and we show how value statements can be developed in an organisation. We conclude this chapter by discussing ethical values in relation to specific stake-holders. Again, company examples are included to sup-port our arguments.

Chapter 6 covers *effective implementation of ethical prin-ciples.* Here we examine processes to turn ethical values into ethical behaviours. We review ways of getting it wrong, and put forward criteria for getting it right, including involving managers and staff at all levels. We argue the need for time for ethical values to be internalised. The roles of the chairman, chief executive and board are analysed, and we consider techniques for monitoring effectiveness, including 'hotlines', the in-company ombudsman, certification systems, and questionnaires.

Chapter 7 – supporting ethics through training – emphasises that employees need to be trained in ethical values. The ethical leader wants people to think for themselves, and training can provide case-study examples to help people understand what ethics is about, and how ethical issues can be resolved. The essential components of effective training in ethics are described.

Chapter 8 examines *the role of HR in business conduct*. The HR function may well be seen as the upholder of the corporate conscience, although HR does not have the sole responsibility in this area. Our view is that ethics must be stimulated, owned and promoted by the board as a whole. However, in this chapter we review a number of areas where the ethical indication of action for HR professionals is significant, including training and development, reward strategies, equal opportunities and communication.

Chapter 9 covers *ethical leadership and strategic choice*. In this chapter we examine how to manage ambiguities. We start by reviewing ethical leadership in respect to life-cycle theory and then we review ethical choices in two principal areas – outcome and process. Throughout this chapter we return to our central theme of integrating ethical values with vision and strategies.

Chapter 10 is our concluding section and defines the *critical success factors for ethical leadership*. We list 14, including the need to align ethical values to vision, the need for visible top-management support and the importance of reinforcing ethical leadership through, for example, communication at all levels.

Conclusions

Throughout this book, we will argue the importance of ethical leadership. In doing so, we recognise that some managers, in the UK in particular, do display a certain caution on the subject of business ethics. Some feel that the existence of an ethics code indicates that there is a problem, which somehow insults the workforce; others feel that an ethics code introduces prescriptions which would constrain business managers from arriving at optimum decisions. Some, more cynically, feel that ethics is just a PR exercise – simply window-dressing.

These are not isolated views. Considering them helps us to keep our feet on the ground in dealing with a sensitive and complex subject. By reviewing the evidence of organisations that have got it wrong, as well as those that have gained competitive advantage through ethical leadership, we will argue for a focus on ethics within the organisation. This 'focus' need not be prescriptive or bureaucratic. Nor is it a 'box', managed by HR or legal – people to blame if it goes wrong. Ethics is for everyone, and for all time.

References

1. *Financial Times*, 24 October 1994, p. 7.
2. Elaine Sternberg in *Just Business*, Warner Books, 1994, adopts this phrase; p. 88.
3. 'Shattered Image' in *Business Ethics*, 1 September 1994.
4. *Sunday Times*, 4 June 1995.
5. Bodo B. Schleselmilch and Jane E. Houston: 'Corporate Codes of Ethics' in *Management Decisions*, Vol. 28, No. 7, 1990, p. 39.
6. Elaine Sternberg, *op. cit.* p. 17.
7. Tom Peters: *Thriving on Chaos*. London, Macmillan, 1987, p. 522.
8. Laura L. Nash 'Why business ethics now?' quoted in *Managing Business Ethics*, Oxford, Butterworth-Heinemann, 1994, p. 11.
9. R. Edward Freeman and Daniel R. Gilbert Jr: *Corporate Strategy and the Search for Ethics*, Hemel Hempstead, Prentice Hall, 1988, p. 17.
10. Cited in Ralph Stacey (ed.), *Strategic Thinking and the Management of Change*, London, Kogan Page, 1993, p. 135.
11. John Collins 'Why bad things happen to good companies – and what can be done', *Business Horizons*, November–December 1990, p. 19.

12. *ibid* p. 20.
13. See, for example, John Donaldson and Peter Davis: 'Business ethics? Yes, but what can it do for the bottom line?' *Management Decision*, 28, 6, 1990, pp. 29–33.
14. Stephen King, 'Brand building and market research' in Mark Jenkins and Simon Know (eds): *Advances in Consumer Marketing*, London, Kogan Page, 1994, p. 122.
15. *ibid* pp.123–124.
16. W. Bennis and B. Nanus, quoted in R. Stacey (ed.) *op. cit.* (see note 10) pp. 140–141.

2

◪ Ethical Issues in Business

Pressures on senior and middle management to achieve business goals are relentless. Cost-cutting initiatives can impact on the profits of an organisation faster, and more surely, than growing the top line. To help companies maintain service standards in the context of cost cutting, business process re-engineering seeks to fundamentally reform working practices, removing unnecessary layers, and simplifying processes.[1] These changes, essential as they are, create new project teams and key staff are seconded to them. This, in turn, adds to operational pressures in the short term.

For organisations that seek to grow volume as well as cut costs, the competitive issues they face will be daunting to all but the most monopolistic of providers. Direct marketing and selling techniques can gain short-term advantage, but customers become immune to endless direct approaches. Price and service will, as always, be predominant features in customers' minds. Price cutting adds to pressures on margins already in the 1990s, eroded by years of recession. Maintaining – enhancing – service standards costs money, too, although here the commercial advantages in the medium and long term are likely to be significant.

Competitive tendering in the public sector, regulatory pressures in the newly privatised utilities and in other sectors such as financial services, add to managerial pressures. As headcount reduces through (generally) voluntary retirement and voluntary severance, so the workload of the remaining workforce can increase, especially if redesign activity has not been undertaken.

This context provides the setting for our analysis of ethical issues in business, including reviewing ethical obligations to shareholders, customers, staff, suppliers, and the community. We begin our review with survey results on ethics.

17

Surveys of views on ethics

The pressures on management referred to above will be commonly felt amongst organisations in the mid-1990s. In this context, ethical standards can be threatened. As one study put it:

> 65% of middle managers . . . felt themselves to be under pressure to compromise their own personal standards in order to achieve the goals of their corporation.[2]

In this survey, the most frequently mentioned pressures are shown in Table 2.1. The significant percentages quantifying 'Pressures to show profits and keep costs in line' and 'Time pressures' will not surprise anyone.

Table 2.1
Pressures on Management[3]

Type of pressure	Responses	Percentage
Pressures to show profits and keep costs in line	56	21.7
Time pressures	39	15.1
Production and sales quotas	25	9.7
Employee relations	21	8.1
Pressures to meet quality standards	16	6.2
Union pressures	14	5.4
Product development	11	4.3
Corporate politics – relations with top management	15	5.8
Upward promotion pressures	7	2.7

Despite these pressures, managers in the UK at least are generally unlikely to place ethics as one of their business priorities. An April 1994 study[4] of almost 100 industrialists and others showed that their top priorities were:

	percentage
• profits/return on investment/financial probity	31
• understanding customers' needs/customer satisfaction	12
• effective/clear strategy	11
• understanding the context in which the business operates	11
• people/motivation/staff quality	10

If ethical behaviour was not considered a top priority for the participants in this survey, other studies also suggest that management do need to focus more on ethical leadership. A Harris Poll in the USA on 3 September 1992 showed 69 per cent of the participants saying that business executives were believed to have unethical standards[5]. In another poll, US business people were asked about acceptable practices and whether they would bend the law in certain circumstances:

> Approximately one-quarter said they would write bad cheques, invade the privacy of job interviewees, pirate software, steal clients, and inflate their sales.[6]

Here we confront the first major issue to be addressed in this chapter. Managers are clearly under great pressure to achieve goals. There are plenty of case-studies revealing scandalous behaviour to show what can go wrong at the extremes: Barlow Clowes, the Bank of Credit and Commerce International (BCCI), Robert Maxwell siphoning money from his company pension funds, and so on.[7] Yet we have often found from our own experience that managers do not feel they *personally* face ethical dilemmas. Indeed, some managers argue that there is no need for an ethical dimension to their leadership, since there are 'no problems here!' The parallel with equal opportunities issues will not be lost on the reader. Similarly, when employees are asked if a code of ethics might be useful, the majority answer 'yes' since they feel it will 'control' their manager, who may be tempted to act unethically. Rarely will it be seen as a mechanism to influence their own behaviour. There is here an apparent gap between ethics in theory and ethics in practice. To understand this better we need to examine in more detail *managerial* perceptions of ethical issues.

Managerial perception of ethics

If managers in the UK are not currently especially focused on business ethics, discussions with managers at all levels and in a variety of commercial sectors reveals a number of important perceptions on the subject which influence behaviour. These are analysed under three headings:

(a) definition of business ethics
(b) examples of unethical behaviour
(c) issues preventing or reinforcing ethical behaviour

We will consider each of these in turn.

(a) *Definition of business ethics*   We have in the Introduction defined ethics as 'about fairness, about deciding what is right or wrong, about defining the practices and rules which underpin responsible conduct between individuals and groups'. When managers are asked the question: 'What is meant by business ethics?', they respond in a number of ways, some of which relate to our definition:

- There is a common emphasis on honesty. Being direct, straightforward and open in their dealings with others were regularly identified as key elements in managing ethically.
- 'Do unto others as you would have them do unto you' is another typical response. Archie Carroll in a 1990 survey of middle managers also identifies this principle.[8]
- Doing things the manager would be comfortable with if they came to light, is a central theme. Would the manager object

to his or her friends and family knowing the circumstances? One company has referred to this as the '*Private Eye* Test' – would they mind if the issue was exposed in *Private Eye*?

- Think about the long term. Consistency and constancy of purpose are major themes in managing ethically. So is avoiding a short-term fix for short-term gain. Customers, suppliers, shareholders, staff – all the different stakeholders value a relationship which is to their long-term benefit. We shall return to this issue in Chapter 4 on 'ethics and vision'.

These are straightforward comments reflecting what managers, who are not philosophers, would say in response to the question: 'What is meant by business ethics?' References to honesty, openness, constancy of purpose and treating others as you would wish yourself to be treated is an attempt to articulate norms, values, and morals which should underpin managerial behaviour. As one recent study put it:

> Norms and values, reasonableness, moral community, equity and reciprocity, obligation, and responsibility are core concepts in ethical practice as well as ethical reflection.[9]

We also draw out the links between ethics and values in Chapter 5.

(b) *Examples of unethical behaviour* Managers find it easier to define examples of unethical behaviour than they do to list examples of ethical behaviour. Here are some of the most frequently quoted examples of unethical behaviour:

- using external subcontractors to provide a service who are less qualified than permanent staff, and who care less about customer service
- giving gifts to a buyer knowing that he or she will be swayed in your favour as a result
- being dishonest – for example telling a customer that work needs to be undertaken when it does not

- theft of any kind
- 'slagging off' the company internally or externally
- selling a product under false pretences – for example, omitting to mention a poor service-history when selling a product
- stealing another person's ideas without giving credit
- reading other people's mail for personal gain
- charging 'soft' customers more than someone whom you believe is 'sharper'
- dismissing someone without a full investigation
- insisting that staff work significantly longer hours than the job requires, without consideration of the individual's personal circumstances
- insider-trading
- giving higher rewards to certain individuals not supported by performance.

Laura Nash identified 30 ethical quandaries reproduced in Table 2.2. To her, these are:

> not hot-house problems that occur once in a career, they are familiar dilemmas. A company has at least twenty on the table every day. A manager has at least twenty on his or her desk every year. What I find equally impressive is their elusive nature. These are the kinds of situations that seem obviously wrong from a distance, but are so embedded in other concerns and environmental circumstances that the demarcations between right and wrong are blurred. Even price-fixing has been regarded by many otherwise high-minded executives as not really significant from a moral standpoint.

> With the possible exception of number 13, each example poses a choice to step over the moral line or not. An ethical resolution to these situations requires discretional judgment about degree, overall goals, immediate logistical problems, other trade-offs, chances of success, and so on. There is no canned program or magical mirror to help you determine what is right and wrong.

> Such dilemmas are at the core of every manager's job, and their resolution rests partly on the foundation of values he

Table 2.2

Familiar ethical quandaries

1. Greed
2. Cover-ups and misrepresentation in reporting and control procedures
3. Misleading product or service claims
4. Reneging or cheating on negotiated terms
5. Establishing policy that is likely to cause others to lie to get the job done
6. Overconfidence in one's own judgment to the risk of the corporate entity
7. Disloyalty to the company as soon as times get rough
8. Poor quality
9. Humiliating people at work or by stereotypes in advertising
10. Lockstep obedience to authority, however unethical and unfair it may be
11. Self-aggrandisement over corporate obligations (conflict of interest)
12. Favoritism
13. Price-fixing
14. Sacrificing the innocent and helpless in order to get things done
15. Suppression of basic rights: freedom of speech, choice, and personal relationships
16. Failing to speak up when unethical practices occur
17. Neglect of one's family, or neglect of one's personal needs
18. Making a product decision that perpetrates a questionable safety issue
19. Not putting back what you take out of the environment, employees, and/or corporate assets
20. Knowingly exaggerating the advantages of a plan in order to get needed support
21. Failing to address probable areas of bigotry, sexism, or racism
22. Courting the business hierarchy versus doing the job well
23. Climbing the corporate ladder by stepping on others
24. Promoting the destructive go-getter who outruns his or her mistakes
25. Failing to cooperate with other areas of the company – the enemy mentality
26. Lying by omission to employees for the sake of the business
27. Making an alliance with a questionable partner, albeit for a good cause
28. Not taking responsibility for injurious practices – intentional or not
29. Abusing or just going along with corporate perks that waste money and time
30. Corrupting the public political process through legal means

Source: Laura L. Nash, *Good Intentions Aside: A managers' guide to resolving ethical problems*, Boston, Mass., Harvard Business School Press, 1990, pp. 8–10. Copyright © 1990, 1993 by the President and Fellows of Harvard College.

or she brings to the task, but also on many conditions beyond a manager's direct control.[10]

The next chapter examines these ethical issues in more depth.

(c) *Perception of issues preventing or reinforcing ethical behaviours*   Saul Gellerman in 'Why "good" managers make bad ethical choices'[11] identifies four commonly held rationalisations that can lead to misconduct:

- a belief that the activity is within reasonable ethical and legal limits
- a belief that the activity is in the individual's or the corporation's best interests
- a belief that the activity is 'safe' because it will never be found out or publicised
- a belief that because the activity helps the company, the company will condone it and even protect the person who engages in it.

Gellerman goes on to say:

> The idea that an action is not really wrong is an old issue. How far is too far? Exactly what is the line between smart and too smart? Between sharp and shady? Between profit maximisation and illegal conduct. The issue is complex: it involves an interplay between top management's goals and middle managers' efforts to interpret these aims.[12]

In making judgements about what is appropriate behaviour or what is unethical behaviour, managers weigh up a vast array of sometimes conflicting policies and top-management statements. The following obstacles can be seen as impacting upon ethical choices:

Job insecurity: An organisation which has introduced compulsory redundancy, or the threat of it, may find staff are insecure. In this context rumours abound, morale is threatened and the cynics in the organisation are listened to first. Not everyone who is insecure may be tempted to care little about customers, to badmouth the organisation or leak data to the press with mischievous intent, or even to sabotage software systems. However, these unethical behaviours are more likely in an organisation where morale is low, and people feel unhappy and insecure.

Performance management: Setting objectives for employees at all levels is a key component of effective business and human resource management. It clarifies job priorities, focuses staff on the right issues, and allows training needs to be more accurately identified. Linking pay fairly and consistently to performance can also be motivating to high performers, and act as a catalyst to others to improve their performance. For these reasons, performance management and performance-related pay are widely practised.[13] However, there are dangers. Objectives can be poorly defined or non-existent. Judgements on pay are then seen as dubious, since the standards for judgement seem subjective. In dynamic organisations objectives do change, and managers should attempt to capture in writing the major changes through the year. Similarly, key objectives should not be impossible to achieve – stretching but realistic. With job reductions and other cost-reduction initiatives dominating the agenda, there may be a temptation to circumvent effective performance management disciplines. Lack of consistency and fairness in performance-related pay can cause widespread dissatisfaction.

Personal ambition: We have all seen examples of the individual whose desire to succeed can affect judgements about right or wrong. Where personal ambition is coupled with a big ego and a natural sycophancy, the ingredients which produce the rationalisations Gellerman refers to above will be in place.

A blame culture: Where staff perceive that a mistake will lead to public reprimands, to a scapegoat being found, to long-term damage to a hitherto promising career, then there may be a tendency to keep quiet. Better to keep your head down and allow unethical practices to pass by than to speak up and be kicked. Such a blame culture does not see mistakes as opportunities for learning. What can be created in this culture is an organisation of sycophants, who privately condemn the top management. Rumours and fears persist in this climate.

Laziness: Often, people know what it is right to do, but don't do it. This may be rationalised as Gellerman suggests or it may be that people just can't be bothered. Often such an attitude reflects other underlying problems of morale referred to above.

'Street cred': Pressures to act in a 'macho' way can be powerful. This can affect top management who may be tempted to break a few rules to impress the Chairman, or to emphasise profits before all else, through to the craftsman who doesn't wear the safety equipment because his colleagues will think him weak.

Uncertainty on standards: There may be ambiguity on what is expected within the organisation. We return to codes of practice in Chapter 7

These are real issues facing organisations today – job insecurity, pressures on objectives leading to unrealistic targets, personal ambition driving behaviour, a tendency to blame others. Managers will relate such elements to 'the organisation', their boss, and less commonly to their staff.

There are, too, actions which reinforce the notion that ethics matters. Some of these have been summarised by Tom Cannon,[14] as shown in Table 2.3, which also includes his views on actions that undermine ethical standards.

Ethical obligation to different stakeholders

Most organisations if asked to list their stakeholders will identify four – shareholders, customers, employees and mem-

Table 2.3
Pressures for and against ethical standards

Undermining ➤◄	Reinforcing
Rewards for quantity over quality	Emphasis on quality
Bottom line pressure for profits at any cost	Clearly formulated ethical standards
Closed door practices and emphasis on secrecy	Fully articulated standards
Punishments for reporting policy violations	Openness
Uncertainty about ethical standards	Frequent and public endorsement of standards
Patterns of deception throughout management	Clear channels of communication on breaches of standards
Emphasis on 'group' loyalty even at expense of others	Standards committees
Group-think	Follow-through
Reluctance to act where problems identified	Reward and recognition systems which emphasise standards
Social bullying	Prompt non-adversarial remedial action
Fear	

Source: Tom Cannon, *Corporate Responsibility*, London, Pitman, 1994, p. 105.

bers of the local community. Some companies – such as Marks & Spencer – would add suppliers. In this chapter on the perception of managers regarding ethics, we use these five stakeholder groupings and examine ethical issues within each category.

Shareholders

Corbetta (1994) identifies the following main types of ownership of medium-sized and large companies:

a. Family-based capitalism: ownership is concentrated in the hands of one or a few families.

b. Financial capitalism: ownership is concentrated in the hands of one or just a few private and public financial institutions.

c. Managerial capitalism: ownership is shared amongst numerous stakeholders, none of whom individually exercises significant control.

d. State capitalism: through agencies or corporations, the state has direct control.[15]

The debate here will concentrate on category (c.) above. Tom Sorell and John Hendry offer the following analysis:

> Whether members or owners, stakeholders can, if their stakes are large enough or if they are persuasive enough, affect the affairs of a company decisively. Because shareholders usually invest in order to collect dividends that they are led by the firm to expect, a firm cannot discharge its obligation to shareholders without attempting to trade profitably. On the other hand the pressures which a firm may be tempted to adopt to cut costs and maximise profits can sometimes include obligations to other groups, e.g. the employees. So one question about shareholders concerns the priority of the obligation to provide them with a good return, and the moral costs of putting this obligation first. To what extent is the obligation overriding?[16]

For these authors, this is the most pressing question for shareholders. Of course, 'shareholders' are not a fixed group – they can sell up and switch investments. Institutional investors may have a longer-term view of their investment. However, the issue here is how conflicting goals between any shareholders and customers or employees can be reconciled. Often, this will necessitate a judgement on how much profit is seen as acceptable to the shareholders, and the nature and extent of the claim of alternative stakeholders – customers, staff, and the local community in particular.

Of course, shareholders as owners of the company elect directors to run the business on their behalf and they are held accountable for its progress. Directors, with legal responsibilities to the shareholders, need to be careful with decisions which dilute shareholder value even where the claims of alternative stakeholders are clear.[17]

For the ethical leader, judgements about shareholder value versus other competing claims bring the debate to the question of purpose. What is the company for? For whose benefit is the effort being put in? There are deep issues here, which we return to in the discussion on vision and ethics in Chapter 4. Each company will need to think through its position. Ethical leadership in this context may involve providing clarity of purpose, and avoiding extreme positions which cannot be justified publicly. As we shall see in Chapter 4, most managers will acknowledge the claims of other stakeholders, such as customers, employees, suppliers, and the community, alongside those of shareholders. As one study of the principles for the high-ethics firm put it:

> Principle 1: High-ethics firms are at ease with diverse internal and external stakeholder groups. The ground rules of these firms make the good of those stakeholder groups part of the firm's own good.[18]

It is Milton Friedman however who argues most persuasively that business corporations have only one social responsibility, and that is to increase their profits. He holds that meeting 'social responsibilities' means reducing returns to stockholders – it is spending their money.

> In a free-enterprise, private-property system, a corporate executive is an employee of the owners of the business. He has direct responsibility to his employers. That responsibility is to conduct the business in accordance with their desires, which generally will be to make as much money as possible while conforming to the basic rules of the society, both those embodied in law and those embodied in ethical customs.[19]

In this robust defence of *laissez-faire* capitalism, the issue of other stakeholders such as customers still raises its head. Friedman does not define these, but alternative interests do need to be considered even by staunch adherents of shareholder-value as the only goal for top management. We now turn to some of these alternative interests.

Customers

One of the major managerial philosophies to achieve widespread acceptance in the 1980s and 1990s has been the importance of the customer, and the need to satisfy – even 'delight' – the customer. Such a focus on internal and external customer satisfaction has led to the adoption of 'total quality management' approaches to improving quality. TQM has been defined as:

> a management philosophy which seeks continuous improvement in the quality of all processes, products and services of an organisation. It emphasises the understanding of variation, the importance of procurement, the role of the customer and the involvement of employees at all levels of the organisation.[20]

Deming's TQM action plan is worth reproducing to demonstrate the main components of this approach (see Table 2.4).

Total quality programmes have refocused management attention to customer requirements, and helped them track the source of customer complaints through detailed root-cause analysis.

Ethical issues abound in this area, including:

- *product safety* – products must meet certain minimum requirements regarding their quality, to avoid personal injury or economic losses, or both.
- *pricing* – judgements are being made by management on pricing policy which will involve detailed consideration of what the 'market' will bear, in relation to the standard of

Table 2.4

Deming's TQM Action Plan

Action must be taken in order to:
1. create purpose constantly for the organisation
2. adopt and understand the never-ending improvement philosophy
3. replace the mass inspection with statistical monitoring of the never-ending improvement of the production process
4. change the philosophy of purchasing of awarding business on the basis of price
5. strive constantly to improve the system rather than blaming workers for the company's problems
6. institute modern methods for training workers
7. focus more on supervisors providing a supportive environment of works
8. drive out fear that employees may have in telling management about problems
9. break down the organisation barriers that exist in today's businesses
10. eliminate arbitrary numerical goals and integrate personal goals with the organisation's overall goal of never-ending improvement of quality
11. replace management by numbers with statistical methods for measuring never-ending quality improvement
12. facilitate and promote pride of workmanship
13. institute extensive education and training at every level of the organisation
14. structure the organisation so that all staff are involved in never-ending quality improvement.

Source: W.E. Deming, *Out of Crisis*, MIT Center for Advanced Engineering Study, Cambridge, MA, 1986.

service being provided, what gross margins are necessary to produce satisfactory trading profits, what the competition are doing, and the PR consequences of different pricing policies. The average customer will have little comparative information on which to base decisions, although through the Consumers' Association and other bodies more information is available to facilitate consumer choice. There is potential for exploitation of 'weak' customers here. The notion of 'best advice' to customers has an ethical foundation, and is seen most clearly in the financial services industry.

- *terms of contract* – the 'small print' on contracts is often an area which can surprise and disappoint customers if there is ever a need to study it.
- *advertising* – relevant and accurate information should be provided to customers to enable them to make an appropriate choice. There is considerable scope for ethical conflict in this area, especially with the use of music, pictures and colours which are suggestive in a way deemed appropriate by the company to support sales. For example:

> The image of a Malboro cigarette is therefore closely attached to the subjective imagination of cowboy adventures, freedom and romance of the great outdoors.[21]

Most managers when considering the ethical issues involved with customers refer to the need for openness and honesty. The concept of 'relationship-selling' is often seen as relevant, with the emphasis on the need to retain a customer long-term.

Staff

Many organisations keen to develop best practice in the field of human resource management have developed high-level principles and practices associated with a quality workforce. These include the following components:

- attracting, developing, motivating, and retaining people of the right calibre who relate to, and identify with, the vision and core values of the organisation
- allowing all staff the opportunity to achieve their full potential
- rewarding staff in relation to achievement, skills and knowledge, market rates and job size
- providing staff with the training and development necessary

to enable them to become fully effective in their current job and achieve their full potential

- implementing open and effective communication, designed especially to generate understanding, acceptance, and commitment to change
- maintaining sound and constructive relationships with staff through involvement and participation at all levels
- being proactive in support of equal opportunities
- providing a safe, well designed, and satisfying working environment.

Each of these elements will be explained in more detail in the next chapter. Underpinning these 'best practice' principles are certain rights and duties both for employees and employers, which have been analysed as shown in Table 2.5.

As well as UK employment legislation, the Maastricht Treaty of 1991 and the European Social Chapter are relevant to the legal basis of employment rights and duties.[22]

As with each component of this stakeholder analysis, numerous ethical issues are perceived by management. These include:

- the problems associated with 'the fair wage'. The earlier part of this chapter touched on the issue of performance management and performance-related pay. On a deeper level there are questions about comparative pay levels: What should be the ratio between the basic pay of unskilled workers and directors in an organisation? The prevalence of stock option schemes in US and UK companies has sharpened the issue, bringing into focus total remuneration as well as basic pay. In the 1990s there has also been a movement away from job evaluation methods to underpin relative pay differences, since they become unwieldy and bureaucratic. However, in their absence, more subjectivity may arise. Pay levels can be related to the relevant labour market to justify differences, and this may be economically necessary. However, grievances can arise internally as people performing like work feel aggrieved at being on different pay rates.

Table 2.5

Employees' and employer's rights and duties

Employees' rights and duties	Employer's rights and duties
• Right to work	• No-discrimination rules for recruitment; conditions for firing
• Right to just remuneration	• Duty to fair compensation
• Right to free association and to strike	• Respect for union presence and activities
• Right to privacy and to normal family life	• Work-oriented code of conduct
• Freedom of conscience, and freedom of speech	• Acceptance of criticism from workers, without repression
• Right to due process	• Acceptance of labour court jurisprudence in conflicts
• Right to participation	• Duty to inform and to consult workers
• Right to healthy and safe working conditions	• Duty to guarantee same
• Right to work quality (job satisfaction)	• Duty to improve quality of work
• Duty to comply with labour contract	• Demand of minimal productivity of employees
• Loyalty to the firm	• Right to loyal co-operation
• Respect for current legal and moral norms	• Requirement of correct behaviour at the workplace

Source: Jef van Gerwen, in Brian Harvey (ed.) *Business Ethics*, Hemel Hempstead, Prentice Hall, 1994, p. 57.

- placing too many burdens on staff, whose domestic lives may then be threatened. How far should an organisation go in this regard?
- positive discrimination. This is a subject which many managers – men and women – regard as unethical and patronising.
- compulsory redundancy. Whilst there can be no absolute guarantee of work in any organisation, most managers feel compulsion should be avoided where possible.
- trade unions. The right to form and join a trade union is a basic employee right, although one that continues to raise deep concerns amongst managers. The issues involve around

loyalty to the employer versus the collective strength that trade unionism inevitably provides to the individual employee.[23]

- maintaining information on employees in strict confidence, even to the individual concerned. Most companies still hold to the view that succession-planning data will be kept confidential, but the 'general file' can be seen by the employee. The Data Protection Act 1984 has opened up information held on computer, although much still remains on paper.
- openness of information. How much information can managers provide to staff? Stock Exchange disclosure rules in relation to insider-dealing are relevant here.
- introducing AIDS-testing in the workplace.[24]

How these matters are dealt with will be the subject of later chapters in this book.

Suppliers

Surprisingly little is to be found in ethics textbooks concerning the issues surrounding suppliers. There are headings to be considered similar to those we reviewed above in the section on customers, but there are some important additional points too. These include:

- paying on time. Smaller companies in particular can be vulnerable to delays in settling invoices. Cash-flow is, of course, a critical dimension for all companies. Managing debtors is in itself a growing specialism.
- fair tendering procedures. Competitive tendering in all sectors of the economy needs to be handled with impartiality and perceived fairness.
- not defaulting on a contract. Having established terms of reference with suppliers, these should be adhered to.
- not abusing the reputation of the client. Sub-contractors

have a responsibility to maintain the image and reputation of the client. Similarly, the client must legally establish the right terms of reference, and monitor them regularly.

Community

There are many ethical questions here raised by managers:

- What is responsible business action towards the environment?[25]
- How 'green' should the business be in relation to, say, disposal of industrial waste, affirming animal rights, consuming energy, protecting the ozone layer, or preserving the countryside?[26]
- What role should business take in relation to the local community, including encouraging onward-investment?
- What role should organisations take in caring for the elderly and disadvantaged in their community, or amongst their customer base?
- What support should organisations provide to sports and to the arts?
- Should organisations support their staff serving in the community?

The environmental issues are the most significant element in this list. The Rio summit highlighted the need for action on the environment.[27]

Two overriding ethical issues

Having analysed ethical conflicts in relation to the different stakeholders – shareholders, customers, staff, suppliers and the community – there are two overriding ethical issues perceived by management which are worthy of brief attention in this final part of the chapter. These are:

- ethics and different cultures
- ethics and negotiating skill

Each will be examined in turn.

Ethics and different cultures

David Vogel in an article in *Business Ethics* in 1993 analysed different national approaches to business ethics. He found that business ethics in the USA has been affected by

> the tradition of liberal individualism that . . . is typical of American culture.[28]

He found more cynicism about the ethics of business in Europe. In part, this was because the moral status of capitalism in Europe has always been somewhat pragmatic. Some Europeans have tended to view the pursuit of profit and wealth as inherently morally dubious, making them less likely to be surprised – let alone outraged – when companies and managers are discovered to have actually been greedy!

In addition, in the USA, federal sentencing guidelines which came into effect in November 1991 doubled the median level of fines for corporations found guilty of crimes such as fraud. The guidelines also said that companies would be treated more leniently if they had previously demonstrated efforts to be good corporate citizens. Ethics codes proliferated as a result.

There is much evidence that business practices which appear to be unethical in one culture are acceptable in others. Complex factors are involved here:

> The emphasis in Japan on the group, for example, contrasts sharply with the individualism which dominates Anglo-Saxon debate on values and responsibilities. In Islam, attitude towards religious observance and social obligation struggle to co-exist with Western materialism. Fate, caste, family and respect play a complex part in shaping the business behaviour of Hindu business.[29]

Ethics and negotiating skill

This is a major area of concern for managers. Ethics, with its emphasis on honesty and openness, does not sit easily with the day-to-day negotiating behaviour of managers. Such issues are not normally perceived as moral ones, but as operational.[30] Managers are paid to deliver an effective purchasing contract, to secure an expert contract on advantageous gross margins, to hold down pay increases. How does this sit with an ethics policy which emphasises 'fairness' and not exploiting weakness in the other side?

Albert Carr in his *Harvard Business Review* article 'Is business bluffing ethical?' sought to deal with these questions:

> If a man plans to take a cent in the business game, he owes it to himself to monitor the principles by which the game is played including the special ethical outlook. He can then hardly fail to recognise that an occasional bluff may well be justified in terms of the game's ethics and warranted in terms of economic necessity . . .
>
> To be a winner, a man must play to win. This does not mean that he must be ruthless, cruel, harsh or treacherous. On the contrary, the better his reputation for integrity, honesty and decency, the better his chances of victory will be in the long run. But from time to time every business-man, like every poker player, is offered a choice between certain loss or bluffing within the legal rules of the game. If he is not resigned to losing, if he wants to rise in his company and industry, then in such a crisis he will bluff – and bluff hard.[31]

The point here is that if both parties know the 'rules of the game' – to use the poker analogy – then it is fair to adopt established negotiating tactics. If however, one side is not playing by these same rules – for cultural reasons, for example, or because of inexperience, it would be unethical to exploit this weakness. Another matter for subtle and complex judgement for the ethical leader.

Summary

This chapter has reviewed the main ethical issues faced by businesses. Relentless pressures on managers mean that many feel their personal ethical standards may be compromised. Ethics is defined in common-sense terms by most managers, and includes concepts such as honesty and openness and doing to others as you would do to yourself. Many ethical quandaries can be listed, although British managers in particular are less focused on issues of social responsibility than on solving day-to-day problems. Ethical judgements are, however, influenced by job insecurity, by a performance-related culture, by personal ambition, and by peer group pressures on 'street-cred'. In this context, different ethical issues arise related to different stakeholders – shareholders, customers, staff, suppliers, the community. Other overriding ethical issues, such as ethics in different cultures and ethics and negotiating skills, create further problems for management.

How these issues are solved through ethical leadership provides the focus for the remaining chapters of this book.

References

1. See Michael Hammer and John Champy, *Re-engineering the Corporation. A manifesto for business revolution*, London, Nicholas Brealey Publishing, 1993.
2. Marshall B. Clinard, *Corporate Ethics and Crime: The role of middle management*, London, Sage Publications, 1983, p. 142.
3. *ibid* p. 92.
4. *Report on Business Ethics* by Opinion Leader Research. Sponsored by KPMG Peat Marwick, Texaco and Whitbread, April 1994 para. 6.4.
5. Quoted in O. C. Ferrell and John Fraedrich, *Business Ethics*, Houghton Mifflin Company, 1994, p. 11.
6. *Ibid* p. 10–11.
7. For a full description of these and other scandals see Tom Sorell and John Hendry, *Business Ethics*, Oxford, Butterworth-Heinemann, 1994, pp. 1–27.

8. Archie Carroll, 'Principles of Business Ethics' in *Management Decision*, Vol. 28, No. 8, 1990, pp. 20–24.
9. Henk van Luijk, 'Business ethics: the field and its importance' in Brian Harvey (ed.), *Business Ethics: A European approach*, Hemel Hempstead, Prentice Hall, 1994, p. 15.
10. Laura L. Nash, *Good Intentions Aside: A manager's guide to resolving ethical problems*, Harvard Business School Press, 1990, pp. 8–10.
11. Saul W. Gellerman, 'Why "good" managers make bad ethical choices' in George D. Chryssides and John H. Kaler, *An Introduction to Business Ethics*, London, Chapman & Hall, 1993, p. 71.
12. *ibid* p. 71.
13. For more details on changing trends in pay see Chris Brewster and Stephen Connock, *Industrial Relations: Cost-effective strategies*, Hutchinson, London, 1985, pp. 82–104.
14. Tom Cannon, *Corporate Responsibility*, London, Pitman Publishing, 1994, p. 105.
15. Guido Corbetta, 'Shareholders' in Brian Harvey (ed.), *Business Ethics: A European approach, op. cit.* pp. 89–90.
16. Tom Sorell and John Hendry, *op. cit.* p. 114.
17. For more analysis of the accountability of boards to shareholders see *Report of the Cadbury Committee on The Financial Aspects of Corporate Governance*, London, Gee Publishing, 1992, pp. 48–52.
18. Mark Pastin, *The Hard Problems of Management: Gaining the ethics edge*, San Francisco, Jossey-Bass Inc., 1986, p. 221.
19. Milton Friedman, 'The social responsibility of business is to increase its profits', *New York Times Magazine*, 13 September 1970, reproduced in George D. Chryssides and John H. Kaler, *op. cit.* (see note 11) p. 249.
20. Alan Brown, 'TQM: implications for training' in *Industrial and Commercial Training*, Vol. 24, No. 10, 1992, p. 3.
21. Eberhard Kuhlmann, 'Customers' in Brian Harvey (ed.), *Business Ethics, op. cit.* (see note 9) p. 109.
22. For more analysis see Tom Sorell and John Hendry, *Business Ethics, op. cit.* (see note 7) pp. 85–112; and Jef van Gerwen, 'Employers' and employees' rights and duties' in Brian Harvey (ed.), *Business Ethics: A European Approach, op. cit.* (see note 9) pp. 56–87
23. See Richard T. De George, 'The right to work: law and ideology', *Valparaiso University Law Review*, 19, Autumn 1994, pp. 15–35;

and Richard T. De George, *Business Ethics*, London, Collier Macmillan, 1990, chapters 15–17.

24. For more detailed analysis of employer–employee issues, including AIDS testing, see Thomas Donaldson and Al Gini, *Case Studies in Business Ethics*, New Jersey, Prentice Hall, 1993 (third edition), p. 110–180.

25. See W. Michael Hoffman,'Business and environmental ethics' in John Drummond and Bill Bain, *Managing Business Ethics*, Oxford, Butterworth-Heinemann, 1994. pp. 152–165.

26. For a useful analysis of this subject see 'The 'greening' of business' in George D. Chryssides and John H. Kaler, *op. cit.* (see note 11) pp. 454–506.

27. Tom Cannon, *op. cit.* (see note 14) p. 249.

28. David Vogel, 'Differing national approaches to business ethics' in *Business Ethics*, Vol. 2, No. 3, July 1993, pp. 164–71.

29. Tom Cannon, *op. cit.* (see note 14) p. 96.

30. For more analysis on this area, see Brian Harvey, Stephen Smith, and Barry Wilkinson, *Managers and Corporate Social Policy: Private solutions to public problems*, London, Macmillan Press, 1984, pp. 127–8.

31. Albert Carr 'Is business bluffing ethical?' *Harvard Business Review*, Jan–Feb 1968, quoted in George D. Chryssides and John H. Kaler, *op. cit.* (see note 11) pp. 117–118.

3

■ Macro-Ethics: Balancing
Priorities

In Chapter 2 we identified the main stakeholders whose
interests need to be considered from an ethical viewpoint. We
concentrated on shareholders, customers, staff, suppliers, and
the community. In this chapter we concentrate on what
organisations are trying to achieve in relation to these stakeholders. Inevitably conflicts arise – how are these to be
reconciled?

Here the inter-relationship between ethical principles and
the organisation's vision, or purpose, is at its most pro-
nounced. As we said in the Introduction, the vision for the
business cannot be considered in isolation from ethical principles.
In pursuing the organisation's purpose, inevitably questions
occur:

- How does pursuit of this purpose affect people and places?
- How does pursuit of this purpose affect me?
- When I take action in pursuit of my purpose, what are the
  short- and long-term consequences for others?

We will argue in this chapter that the key to balancing what
we call those *macro-ethical* issues is to develop a cohesive
vision for the organisation which meets a number of agreed
ethical principles. Inevitably, these are 'big picture' issues
which are the accountabilities of senior management. Issues
affecting all managers and staff we call *micro-ethics*, and these
are reviewed in detail in Chapter 4.

Business goals – balancing stakeholders' expectations

Businesses are profit-seeking organisations, and typically corporate objectives will be defined in terms of profit maximisation.

Difficulties arise immediately. How are profits defined? What is meant by profit maximisation? Should future necessary capital expenditure plans be scrapped in order to gain short-term profit advantage? Similarly, a business must grow for long-term survival. Growth in market-share will often mean a short- or medium-term reduction in profits. The company could reduce its margins, recruit more sales staff, invest in product development, or take on a wide variety of other often costly initiatives to attempt to grow volume. None of these actions will maximise profit in the short term.

So much for a simple view of the goal of a company as 'maximising profits'. Another issue immediately arises which goes to the heart of the issue of balancing stakeholder expectations: what is the right balance between profits and returns to shareholders on the one hand, and prices and customer service levels on the other? Answers to this difficult question partly involve judgements about what price the market will bear, and partly about the gross margins necessary to cover the cost of capital, sales costs, overhead costs, and so on. Macro-ethical issues inevitably arise if 'excessive' gross profit margins are secured by higher prices, or by lower service standards, or both. This can quickly lead to customer dissatisfaction. Arguably, in a perfect market the customer will buy elsewhere. This may not always be possible if, for example, the product has a relative monopoly or if the customer has limited access to competitive information or alternative sources of supply.

Tom Sorell and John Hendry in a perceptive analysis of the ethical issues revolving around different stakeholders, including shareholders, put it this way:

> . . . the measures that a firm may be tempted to adopt to cut costs and maximise profits can sometimes violate obligations to other groups, e.g. the employees. So one question about shareholders concerns the priority of the obligation to provide them with a good return, and the moral costs of putting this obligation first.[1]

Shareholders – we are thinking here mainly of institutional

investors – will have certain expectations for dividend growth, and if these expectations are not met investors could switch their allegiance with consequences for the share price of the company concerned. To avoid this downward trend, management may accelerate cost-reduction actions to improve profitability, thereby maintaining or improving dividends, preferring this strategy to reducing dividend cover. Actions to improve profitability, such as cost-cutting, could have a significant impact on employees if job losses are involved. There are many assumptions in this example, but the point can still be made that priorities have to be weighed very carefully. Table 3.1 shows some fairly common conflicts between stakeholder groups.

Table 3.1
Some common conflict areas

- In order to grow, short-term profitability, cash flow and pay levels may need to be sacrificed.
- When family businesses grow, the owners may lose control if they need to appoint professional managers.
- New developments may require additional funding through share issues or loans. In either case financial independence may be sacrificed.
- Public ownership of shares will require more openness and accountability from the management.
- Cost efficiency through capital investment can mean job losses.
- Extending into mass markets may require decline in quality standards.
- In public services a common conflict is between mass provision and specialist services (eg preventive dentistry or heart transplant).
- In public services savings in one area (eg social security benefits) may result in increases elsewhere (eg school meals, medical care).

Source: Gerry Johnson and Kevan Scholes, *Exploring Corporate Strategy*, Hemel Hempstead, Prentice Hall, 1988, p. 124.

Another analysis of the demands which different stakeholders place on firms is shown in Table 3.2.

Table 3.2

Stakeholders and their expectations

	Expectations	
Stakeholder	*Primary*	*Secondary*
Owners	Financial return	Added value
Employees	Pay	Work satisfaction, training
Customers	Supply of goods and services	Quality
Creditors	Creditworthiness	Security
Suppliers	Payment	Long-term relationships
Community	Safety and security	Contribution to community
Government	Compliance	Improved competitiveness

Source: Tom Cannon *Corporate Responsibility*, London, Pitman Publishing, 1994, p. 45.

The stakeholders defined in Table 3.2 all present different and potentially conflicting expectations to the organisation. The 'owners' may not, of course, be the same as the managers and therefore 'management' could usefully be added to this list. Management may have a primary expectation of securing the long-term viability of the organisation. Shareholders can – and often do – invest for short-term capital or dividend growth and then move on, whereas the management will of necessity need to plan for the long term. Management and owners will have parallel expectations for satisfactory financial returns, and incentives for management such as earnings-per-share bonus schemes and share options can add focus to growth in the relevant financial indicators.

Achieving excellent customer service – viewed in terms of supply of goods and services and quality – is a powerful way to improve profitability. As noted in Chapter 2, most organisations have in the 1980s and 1990s invested in improving the quality of their products and services. Indeed 'total quality management' programmes have become ubiquitous in major organisations. These seek to think through the customers' requirements, and to then exceed such requirements. TQM programmes can cut costs, too, through eliminating unnecessary repetition activities.

The focus on continuous improvement which is at the core of TQM thinking keeps the momentum going, especially if allied to empowerment strategies.

Employees are another stakeholder whose interests are not necessarily homogeneous. Professional staff, for example, may be more interested in job satisfaction and personal growth than industrial staff, where the scope for personal initiatives may be more limited. Nevertheless, expectations for a fair reward related to contribution, for the relevant training to do this job competently, for information about the business, and for job stability are likely to be foremost.

Definitional difficulties exist for the 'community' stakeholder. Is this the people living and working in the vicinity of the organisation? Is it all of us? For national organisations, the community may well be all of us. For regional companies, a narrower definition of the community may be appropriate, much depending on the product or service with which the organisation is involved, and the geographical location of the organisation.

Organisations will need to think through these definitional difficulties when considering their vision for the future. Problems of this kind have led to criticism of the stakeholder approach to considering macro-ethics issues. We now turn to those criticisms, and to alternative methods of analysis.

Problems with stakeholder theory

John Argenti, in his 1993 book *Your Organisation: What is it for?*,[2] argues that if stakeholder theory implies that organisations must work for the common good of all stakeholding participants, it is completely wrong. Indeed, he avoids the term 'stakeholder' because it implies that different people have a stake in the organisation and are therefore in some way *entitled* to a benefit from it.

Eight problems associated with 'stakeholder theory' can be identified, as follows:

- The presence of multiple stakeholders does not add to the legitimacy of the corporation as some commentators have suggested. Organisations could justify themselves merely by demonstrating that they have one beneficiary.
- It is hard to agree on who the stakeholders are. As we have noted above, managers, employees, and customers are closely linked to the organisation and have a profound interest in its future. Yet many employees, for example, do not have such long-term involvement or commitment: they come and go. Some customers perform only a single, fleeting transaction with the organisation. As we have said, some shareholders act as short-term speculators, with no long-term commitment to the company. Are there, as a consequence, shades of stakeholder depending on the depth and/or longevity of the individual's contact with the organisation? Where is (or should be) the cut-off, if there is one? Should there be 'associate' stakeholders?

  Many suppliers can be more dependent on the organisation than its employees or its customers, yet the explicit inclusion of 'suppliers' (either in general or with reference to specific suppliers) as a stakeholder seems to depend on the priorities of the company concerned. Sainsburys, for example, in their company handbook only lists four stakeholders – the local community, the customer, its employees, and shareholders; Marks & Spencer does include suppliers as stakeholders.

  Very rarely will organisations list their bankers, auditors, competitors, the Inland Revenue, and Customs & Excise or the Government as stakeholders. Yet these may have a claim on resource allocation and may be affected by the organisation's actions.
- It is hard to agree what additional rights should be granted to stakeholders. Should stakeholder-employees receive extra

salaries or enjoy more job security than temporary (non-stakeholder) employees? Should extra discounts be offered to stakeholder-customers? In fact, of course, some organisations would supply affirmative responses to both these questions. Japanese companies have historically given exceptional levels of job security to their 'inner circle' staff, not extending to people working on the periphery. Some organisations in the UK still pay from incremental scales, thereby rewarding long service and loyalty, with additional benefits on completion of, say, 25 years of continuous service. Retail organisations in particular seek to tie their customers to them more closely through 'membership' systems and 'loyalty discounts'.

In practice, not only do stakeholders receive varying levels of benefit, depending on the largesse of the organisation, but also some stakeholders are manifestly favoured more than others. This brings us back to how stakeholder expectations can be reconciled.

- Stakeholders do not have common aims and objectives. As we noted when reviewing business goals at the beginning of this chapter, the purposes of various stakeholders are sometimes irreconcilable or even diametrically opposed. When a charity raises its employees' salaries, the beneficiaries suffer; when a company raises its prices, the shareholders may be pleased (assuming it works through to profit and dividends) and the customers upset.
- The role of managers as stakeholders. As we have seen already, there are no agreed rules for the distribution of the benefits (profits) secured by the organisation.

  Conflicts can arise in relation to the role of management. For example:
  - Managers may be awarded significant bonuses even when profits are falling.
  - Managers may 'fight for the company's independence' against a bid, when they should be accepting it in the best long-term interests in relation to maximising shareholder value. Indeed, managers may pay lip-service to their role

in relation to shareholders, while in fact acting in their own self-interest.
- Government ministers may fight for larger budgets even when the 'public good' requires a reduction (for example, sustaining large defence expenditure after the end of the Cold War).

- What is 'the community'? BP spent £18m on 'community programmes' in 1992. This is a huge sum by charitable standards in Britain. From this figure, and others like it, it is clear that the 'community' is becoming a focus of attention as a stakeholder. Cynics may say it is promoted for PR purposes, possibly in an effort to prepare public opinion for the environmental vulnerabilities of the organisation. A less cynical interpretation sees organisations prepared to add value to the community by sponsorship programmes which improve the environment.

- Stakeholder theory obscures the focus on profit and reduces the obligation to be judged by results. Because balancing conflicting stakeholder priorities is a complex issue of judgement, there is a possibility for fudge and compromise detracting from clear accountability for results.

- As a result, stakeholder theory can produce managerial confusion. Uncertainty can be created about what people are supposed to be doing. Worse, it can lead to an organisation being run, by default, for the benefit of whomever is in a position to influence its decisions (most often the managers themselves). Thus, some colleges are run to please education officials; hospitals are run to please consultants; charities exist for the benefit of governors; and research laboratories operate for the benefit of their scientists.

Replacing stakeholder theory

Argenti goes on to suggest two models for acceptable corporate conduct instead of stakeholder theory. Firstly the 'no harm' principle. Secondly, the 'principle of engagement'. We review each in turn.

The 'no harm' principle

At its simplest, this principle provides that no organisation should knowingly cause any significant harm to any of its interest groups. The proposition stated in this way contains certain crucial words and phrases: 'Interest group' means any person or group coming into contact with the organisation: shareholders, customers, employees, the local community, tax collectors, suppliers, and so forth. 'Knowingly' means that we might excuse an organisation which did us harm if we were satisfied that its officials could not reasonably be expected to know that their actions might be injurious. So we would not normally condemn a company's actions if:

- previous similar actions had not caused any significant harm
- an established code of practice had been followed
- the perpetrator had taken reasonable care.

'Significant' reflects the fact that sometimes a degree of 'harm' may be unavoidable. For example, it would be better if a company did not pollute the environment at all – but if the company concerned is a chemical company, it is difficult to see how pollution could be totally avoided unless it were to close down completely. So there are three possible courses of action:

- stop all pollution – by installing new equipment and/or by reformulating to achieve 'clean' production
- clearing up the mess when any does occur
- compensating the victims – the principle of 'the polluter pays' and 'full social-cost pricing' is entirely in accordance with the 'no harm' ethic.

The 'no harm' rule does not, however cater for every

corporate scenario. Sometimes organisations – and especially government – legitimately act in breach of the 'no harm' guidelines when they impose penalties and punishments on citizens for wrongdoing. Also, companies may deliberately seek to damage a competitor in order to reduce its effectiveness, or even to drive it out of business. We can see this in operation among newspapers or in the airline industry. Finally, dismissing employees undoubtedly causes injury but is accepted as an inevitable concomitant of the employment process. The pain can be made more bearable with compensation, however, and assistance with re-employment, and with the knowledge that reasonable procedures have been reasonably followed.

The value of the 'no harm' principle lies in its verifiable simplicity. If an organisation suspects that it is causing damage to anyone then, so the theory goes, it must either desist, or neutralise the damage, or offer full compensation.

The principle of engagement

The principle of engagement turns stakeholder theory on its head: it is an entirely pragmatic, as opposed to ethical, code of behaviour – it is the principle of self-interest, or, as we called it in Chapter 1, tactical ethics, brought up to date. The principle of engagement invites managers

> positively, actively and systematically to reach out to anyone who can contribute to the success of their organisation and deliberately enlist their enthusiastic help, to immerse them, to delight them, in delivering more and more benefit to the organisation's beneficiaries.[3]

Applying this principle firstly to employees, the sole criterion for effective human resource management becomes the extent to which it results in maximum benefit for the organisation's intended beneficiaries – no, not to the employees (that is what stakeholder theory requires), but to the *beneficiaries*.

The principle of engagement suggests that the 'community' should be treated in whatever way best engages its enthusiasm for the greater good of the organisation's beneficiaries. If making donations to local charities, serving on local committees, sponsoring local teams, are going to do that more effectively for a company, then that is the way the company should behave. Of course, in this instance stakeholder theory and engagement theory would lead to virtually identical conclusions and action: but such convergence is by no means inevitable or compulsory.

In comparing stakeholder theory with alternative theories, the following points can be made by way of summary. Stakeholder theory does not tell us who may legitimately claim to be a stakeholder, what they may claim, and who should decide whether to give it to them. Stakeholder theory also can confuse managers; the aims of the organisation become more diffuse; executives take their eyes off the ball because they forget whose interests they are supposed to be serving. Single-mindedness is systematically discouraged, leaving the organisation as 'all things to everybody'.

The 'no harm principle' has the benefit of simplicity, and the principle of engagement is at least pragmatic. We adopt the approach of developing a coherent, long-term vision as the method of reconciling the conflicting claims of different interest groups. We now turn to the importance of vision.

The importance of vision

To us, the principle of engagement seems essentially to assert the primacy of shareholders as the intended beneficiary of private-sector organisations. This cannot remove the need to think through and reconcile the inevitable conflicting demands of alternative stakeholders. If this confuses managers, or leads to dilution of single-minded performance measures, then steps must be taken to clarify the position. This is where the discussions leading to a definition of the organisation's vision and values are so important. The ethical leader will want to develop a framework for action within the organisation, including articulating the core purpose of the business and defining the values which will guide the behaviour of people in the organisation. This chapter concentrates on vision and ethics: Chapter 5 examines values and ethics.

Tom Peters has defined vision as:

> . . . aesthetic and moral – as well as strategically sound. Visions come from within – as well as from outside. They are personal – and group-centred. Developing a vision and values is a messy, artistic process. Living it consciously is a passionate one beyond any doubt.[4]

An organisation's vision (or mission – for our purposes we see the terms as synonymous) will have some of the following characteristics. It will

- be cohesive, providing a common thread through the business and functional strategies
- be inspiring, providing motivation
- be energising, spurring action and commitment
- clarify, providing direction while remaining general enough to remain relevant despite changing short-term conditions
- be simple, communicating a clear concise message about priorities.[5]

Guy Kawasaki suggests that a vision 'acts as a lantern, an anchor, and at times, a conscience'; in his view, a good vision statement exhibits three qualities:

Brevity and simplicity – making it easier to understand and recall. The Girl Scouts have a mission statement which satisfies this requirement: 'to help a girl reach her highest potential'.

Flexibility – so that it can last long-term. 'Ensuring an adequate supply of water' is rigid and confining; the Macintosh [of Apple Computer] Division's mission statement is 'To improve the creativity and productivity of people', which can accommodate computers, laser printers, software, books and training for a long time.

Distinctiveness – differentiating one organisation from another.[6]

Arguably, too, the vision statement can incorporate a higher purpose for the organisation rather than a single objective such as 'rate-of-return-to-shareholders'. At its best, the vision statement will help promote a strong level of commitment among employees, suppliers, customers and shareholders.

Andrew Campbell and Sally Yeung concluded that

> Managing mission is, therefore, a continuous, ongoing process. Few companies will be able to articulate the behaviour standards that drive their mission without working out the problem over a number of years. By being clear about the need to have a mission, the need to create a relationship between strategy and values and the need to articulate behaviour standards, managers can avoid a superficial attitude to mission and continue the analysis thinking and experimentation for long enough to develop the mission that will build a great company.[7]

We agree with this, but we also need to keep our feet on the ground. This was the mission statement for Maxwell Communications plc when it was headed by Robert Maxwell:

> We aim, by excellence of management and pre-eminence in technology, to group the great opportunities created by the ever-increasing worldwide demand for information, prosperity and peace.

What the vision tells us

Vision statements are important as much for what they don't say as for what they actually contain. As Johnson and Scholes point out, such statements can be open or closed. By 'open' they mean general, unmeasured and aspirational; closed statements can be measured and specific and therefore it is possible to say they can be achieved at some future time.[8] Vision statements can also be focused on one stakeholder. All decisions in this context must be assessed against the yardstick of shareholder value. Other companies will focus just on customers or just on employees in their vision. Alternatively, the claims of multi-stakeholders can be acknowledged in the vision.

As indicated above, statements of vision can often involve three dimensions:

- type of purpose
- measurement of success
- definition of competitive arena.

Some statements can include components of all three dimensions, as shown in Table 3.3.

Table 3.3
Consideration for developing a vision

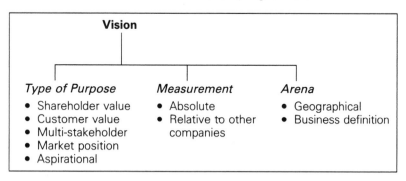

Under types of purpose, examples can be provided as follows:

(a) Shareholder value

> **Hanson** 'We aim to enhance shareholder value by increasing earnings per share and dividends.'

> **Boots** 'Our objective is to maximise shareholder value of the company for the benefit of its shareholders.'

> **3i** 'Its objective is to achieve consistent, long-term capital growth in the value of its portfolio and to distribute an attractive dividend to shareholders.'

Although these examples have an absolute measurement, some can be relative, for example:

> **General Mills** 'Our commitment is to achieve financial results that place us within the top decile of all major companies'.

(b) Customer value

> **Motorola** 'To achieve total customer satisfaction – providing innovative products before they even know they want them.'

> **Nordstrom** 'Our number one goal is to provide outstanding customer service.'

> **Eagle Star** 'We believe that serving the customer is central to the future of Eagle Star.'

> **Courtaulds** 'We aim to meet customers' needs faster, better, more distinctively than the international competition.'

The Courtaulds example above introduces a relative measurement. The following example defines the business arena, too:

> **BUPA** 'To deliver the "best value" independent health financing and insurance.'

(c) Multi-stakeholder

Ferranti 'To develop a performance culture that will provide satisfaction to our shareholders, our customers and our employees.'

Cadbury Schweppes 'Our task is to build on our tradition of quality and value to Schweppes: provide brands, products, financial results and management performance that meet the interests of our shareholders, consumers, employees, customers, suppliers and the Communities in which we operate.'

Federal Express 'People, service, profit.'

John Lewis Patnership 'Our purpose is to secure the fairest possible sharing, among all those who work in it, of all the advantages of ownership.'

(d) Market position

British Airways 'To be the world's favourite airline.'

BT 'To become the most successful world-wide telecommunications group.'

BICC 'To achieve market leadership in its major businesses of cables, and construction, and in related systems and electronics activities'.

Fullers 'We aim to be the best-known, most highly regarded regional brewer.'

AMEC 'To ensure that the group can offer any construction and engineering service the customer needs and that every service offered will be the best in its market.'

All these examples include relative measures and a business or geographical arena.

(e) Aspirational

Body Shop 'Products that don't hurt animals or the
environment.'

Laura   'To establish an enduring relationship with
Ashley   those that share a love of the special lifestyle
that is Laura Ashley.'

Marks &   'Quality, value, service, worldwide.'
Spencer

Glaxo   'The discovery, development, manufacture
and marketing of safe, effective medicines of
the highest quality.'

Each organisation will need to think through its vision,
considering its purpose, the basis to measure success, and the
business or geographical arena within which it operates.
Review of vision can – and should – involve large numbers of
managers and staff to harness different contributions and gain
commitment.

Once the vision is defined as a guiding principle for the
group, business unit purposes can be developed consistent with
the group purpose. These would provide more detail and
greater focus on the precise business situation, and would
include definition of the business or geographical arena.
Beyond this, strategic objectives and annual performance
targets can be defined. These are all key components of the
company's performance management cycles. In this cohesive
way, the vision can become directly translated to individual
performance objectives throughout the business.

We now need to turn to how this definition of vision can be
aligned to ethical principles.

Vision and ethics

Freeman and Gilbert in *Corporate Strategy and the Search for
Ethics* identify a basic assumption about corporate strategy:

Corporate strategy must reflect an understanding of the ethical nature of strategic choice.[9]

They identify four standard questions:

- Where are we going?
- How do we get there?
- What is the blueprint for action?
- How do we measure or control progress?

Linking such basic questions to ethics, the authors suggest answers to the following additional questions:

- *Who is affected by the chosen strategy?* Shareholders, customers, employees, government, suppliers, local communities, competitors and many others will be either harmed or benefited. Ethics is about judging the effects of actions on identifiable individuals and groups.
- *What are the harms and benefits to each stakeholder?* For this, we need a detailed account of the needs, wants, desires and values of each stakeholder group. We would need to know the interests of each group, its purposes and projects.
- *Who is entitled to benefits?* This brings us back to the earlier analysis of stakeholder rights.
- *How do we make decisions about priorities?* As we have said many times, viewpoints will conflict. What is the organisation's priority?[10]

Archie Carroll has also injected ethical consideration into consideration of business principles. He develops the 'principles approach'. Here managers compare their proposed actions, decisions or behaviours with certain principles of ethics. Eleven ethical principles are defined in Table 3.4.

To secure some insights into which of these principles are more attractive to managers, a representative sample was asked to rank these eleven guidelines in terms of the usefulness of each. The *Golden Rule* was ranked highest. The key to this

Table 4

Ethical principles

Principle	Name of principle
1. You should not adopt principles of action unless they can, without inconsistency, be adopted by everyone else.	*Categorical imperative*
2. Individuals should act to further their self-interests so long as they do not violate the law.	*Conventionalist ethic*
3. Do unto others as you would have them do unto you.	*Golden rule*
4. If it feels good, do it.	*Hedonistic ethic*
5. If you are comfortable with an action or decision after asking yourself whether you should mind if all your associates, friends, and family were aware of it, then you should act or decide.	*Disclosure rule*
6. You do what your 'gut feeling' tells you to do	*Intuition ethic*
7. If the end justifies the means, then you should act.	*Means-ends ethic*
8. You should take whatever advantage you are strong enough and powerful enough to take without respect for ordinary social conventions and laws.	*Might-equals-right ethic*
9. This is an age of large-scale organisations – be loyal to the organisation.	*Organisation ethic*
10. You should do only that which can be explained before a committee of your professional peers.	*Professional ethic*
11. You should follow the principle of 'the greatest good for the greatest number'.	*Utilitarian principle*

Source: Archie B. Carroll, 'Principles of business ethics', *Management Decision*, 1990, p. 21.

principle is impartiality and we are encouraged not to make an exception of ourselves: if we want to be treated fairly, then we should treat others fairly. This moral rule is straightforward and easy to understand; motives for endorsing it may appear to be altruistic but are actually a reflection of precautionary, defensive, self-interest.

The *Disclosure Rule* (a clear application of social ethics – see

Chapter 1) also attracts strong support as it moves the focus on to how others, whose opinions you respect, would regard your decisions, actions or behaviour. Ethically, you are on a sound footing if you are still comfortable with your decision after your family and friends have examined it. Undoubtedly, as Chapter 2 made clear when discussing the '*Private Eye* test', the concept of public exposure is a powerful tool, and though it does not provide a cast-iron assurance that you are acting ethically, it does give a strong indication of how a strategy or decision is likely to be viewed.

Gut feeling, or the *Intuition Ethic*, was the third-ranked principle. This departs from any attempt at rational thought, in favour of being driven by one's quick and immediate insight. Surprisingly, the *Utilitarian Principle* – the greatest good for the greatest number – was ranked last. Perhaps this is because it is somewhat abstract, although as a concept it is idealistic and attractive.

The process of strategic review

The link between vision and ethics can therefore be driven by answering certain key questions during the process of strategic review. The distinctive phases in developing a vision with an ethical dimension can be summarised as follows:

1. Conduct a strengths–weaknesses–opportunities–threats (SWOT) analysis of current business strategies.
2. Define critical success factors for the future, including subjects such as:
   • market share
   • profitability
   • investment return
   • customer service standards
   • HR
   • image
   • legal/regulatory

3. Define the key business drivers. An example of such drivers is shown in Table 3.5.

Table 3.5 *Key Business drivers – some examples*

- Achieving to the profit and capital usage plan
- Increasing sales effectiveness
- Developing existing and new customer relationships
- Improving our performance management and control
- Proactive product management
- Managing our reputation
- Shorter cycle times
- Effective use of IT
- People development and training
- Managing the capacity for change

4. Develop vision and strategic objectives from this analysis.
5. Test the emerging vision against the ethical principles defined above.
6. Define performance indicators, to judge progress over time.

Developing the vision and strategic objectives, and assessing them in relation to ethical principles, will be strengthened by the involvement of key managers in the organisation. Such participation provides more opportunity for ethical issues to be revised from different perspectives in the business, and will strengthen commitment to the end product. Of course, in this process, conflicts of interest could – probably will – arise. We now turn to how these conflicts can be best dealt with.

Managing conflicts of interest

The commitment of top-level managers to the organisation's vision or values statement, and to the consequential action implications, is a critical element for their successful implementation. Not only must the commitment be explicit, it also has to be unanimous: so it is preferable for conflicts of interest to be articulated and discussed while the vision is still in its formative stage.

Advocacy by the managing director, chairman, and other top executives of the implementation of the company's corporate principles is a critical element. Such cohesive advocacy from the top strengthens the reputation of the company, both internally and externally, especially as strong leadership includes applying continuous pressure on lower levels of management to maintain their interest in successfully implementing the vision. Leadership by top executives is hollow if corporate bosses fail to set examples themselves by paying only lip-service to the vision and ethical principles.

Adherence to any vision or code of core values will normally be monitored through some sort of adjudicatory system which processes instances of conspicuous compliance (for recognition purposes) and non-compliance (for correction purposes). In most companies, the seniority of the individual(s) concerned will determine which management level will adjudicate on the conflict of interest. At director level it is essential to establish a climate in which individual directors will discuss actual or potential conflicts of interest with the managing director and/or chairman well before the point where decisions are being made on the issues concerning the conflict of interest.

Creation of such a climate presupposes that directors can be made to subscribe to the ethic of the 'Disclosure Rule'. Moreover, they need to be persuaded that if the ethics of a situation creates doubt in their minds, then this doubt should be expressed rather than concealed – much as life assurance proposal forms ask open-ended questions about 'any other pertinent information', without specifying what information they have in mind, and whether any particular piece of information is likely to be 'pertinent' or not.

The appointment of effective, non-executive directors is an additional mechanism for coping with balancing conflicting expectations because such directors are well placed to judge where the balance should lie when there is tension between stakeholders or between the preferences of individual directors and the actions being taken by the company.

Summary

We began by defining macro-ethics as focusing on significant issues for the organisation. This was analysed in relation to the demands of stakeholders, including shareholders, customers, employees, suppliers, and 'the community'. There are difficulties in reviewing stakeholder theory. However the 'no harm' rule and the 'engagement principle' have their own definitional difficulties. The conflicts of interest apparent in reviewing macro-ethical influences can be reconciled through defining a vision for the organisation. This will not only clarify, it will energise and motivate. We reviewed many different approaches to defining vision, including the focus on single stakeholders, or multi-faceted approaches. We then linked vision firmly to ethics particularly through the application of the 'eleven ethical principles'. A process of strategic review which brought out the key macro-ethical issues was advanced.

Having an organisational vision is, however, only one part of the approach of the ethical leader. We also need values to be clarified, and then an infrastructure of training and monitoring to ensure successful implementation. These aspects are covered in the following chapters, beginning with values.

References

1. Tom Sorell and John Hendry, *Business Ethics*, Oxford, Butterworth-Heinemann, 1994, p. 114.
2. John Argenti, *Your Organisation: What is it for?* Maidenhead, McGraw Hill, 1993, p. 36.
3. *ibid* p. 193.

4. Tom Peters, *Thriving on Chaos: Handbook for a management revolution*, London, Macmillan, London, 1989, p. 401.
5. For more details see Stephen Connock, *HR Vision*, London, IPM, 1991.
6. See Guy Kawasaki, *Selling The Dream*, London, HarperCollins, London, 1991.
7. Andrew Campbell and Sally Yeung, 'Creating a sense of Mission', in *Long-Range Planning*, Vol. 24, No. 4, 1991, p. 20.
8. Gerry Johnson and Kevan Scholes, *Exploring Corporate Strategy*, Hemel Hempstead, Prentice Hall, 1988, pp. 113–115.
9. R. Edward Freeman and Daniel R. Gilbert Jr, *Corporate Strategy and the Search for Ethics*, New Jersey, Prentice Hall, 1988, p. 13.
10. *ibid* pp. 46–47.

4

⊞ Micro-Ethics – The Practical Agenda

In the previous chapter we reviewed how priorities are defined and conflicts resolved through the development and implementation of a vision embracing ethical principles. These help 'big picture' issues associated with the primacy of shareholders or customers, the role of the community and other factors. Ethical leadership operates at a micro-level too. This is where 'micro-ethics' arises. By micro-ethics we mean the main day-to-day ethical dilemmas that most managers will face in the workplace. They will, for example, deal with issues like maintaining confidentiality, receiving gifts or hospitality, or using sub-contracted labour. Most managers will not be managing ethical questions associated with the balance between dividends to shareholders or lower prices to customers, or with the organisation's response to global warming. Ethical leadership requires attention to both macro-ethics and micro-ethics.

Micro-ethics – identifying the issues

As we will say many times in this book, it is the day-to-day behaviour of managers and staff in dealing with a diverse range of ethical dilemmas which is fundamental to ethical leadership. We identified some of those ethical dilemmas in the last chapter and also the need for a vision to reconcile such differences. Here we assess how the organisation identifies the main day-to-day ethical subjects which concern managers and staff at all levels. After assessing the ethical 'agenda', we will review in some detail how organisations set the operational framework within which managers and staff can be more certain of behaving ethically.

There are two main ways of assessing the ethical agenda.

66

- Interviews and focus group discussions with managers and staff
- Conducting an ethical audit or climate questionnaire

The first approach is relatively straightforward and involves asking managers and staff basic questions to explore their perceptions of the subject of ethics. The questions could include:

- How do you define ethics?
- How do you differentiate between ethics and values?
- Have you had any dilemmas in recent years which you would define as ethical?
- What problems might arise in dealing with these dilemmas?
- What would you do if you personally faced the following situations:
    being offered a crate of wine by a consultant who wants work from you?
    being invited with your spouse to a top-quality hotel for the weekend by a supplier of the company?
    being asked by someone for confidential information about the company 'as a favour'?
    (Other examples can be provided.)
- Are you clear about company policy in areas related to business ethics?
    (Explore area of ambiguity.)

Such discussions inevitably provide useful information to the company and provide individuals with a sense that they are involved in shaping the organisation's response to issues of business conduct. Managers and staff will also find it helpful to think through certain ethical pointers to clarify their own standards and values. We prefer face-to-face discussions rather than sending out a questionnaire, since this subject, more than most, requires probing and explanation.

The second approach – conducting some form of ethical audit – can be undertaken either (a) as a general 'ethical climate' assessment, (b) as an exercise to test the ethical implications of particular decisions, or (c) as a test of personal business ethics.

Each will be explained in turn.

(a) *Ethical questionnaire*   Table 4.1 shows one approach to an ethical climate questionnaire.

Such a questionnaire can give a snapshot of participants' responses to these issues. It would be interesting to compare and contrast responses to the questions across different functions in the company. For example, what differences would emerge from comparing responses to the statement 'Everyone is expected to stick by the company rules and procedures' from, say, the sales department and the engineering department? Overall conclusions can also be drawn about the style and characteristics of managers and staff in the organisation.

In one study, this questionnaire was used to assess the ethical climate from 872 respondents representing four organisations. Different ethical climates were invoked, such as an 'instrumental climate' – emphasising self-interest and company profit, or a 'caring climate' which focused on friendship, team interest, and social responsibility. As the authors put it:

> Questionnaire results are intended to provide management with an assessment of what the ethical climate of the organisation is at the time when the questionnaire is administered. Management can then determine whether the firm's ethical climate fits with their personal values, and with the strategic aims of the company.[1]

Alan Weiss places a similar importance on ethical audits:

> Senior management should make organisational-ethics assessment and management as serious and routine an undertaking as that of evaluating sales projections, financial status or product quality.[2]

Inevitably, care needs to be taken with such a high-profile view on ethical questionnaires. The information is inevitably

Table 4.1
Ethical Climate Questionnaire

We would like to ask you some questions about the general climate
in your company. Please answer the following in terms of how it
really is in your company, not how you would prefer it to be.
Please be as candid as possible; remember, all your responses
will remain strictly anonymous.

Please indicate whether you agree or disagree with each of the
following statements about your company. Please use the scale
below and write the number which best represents your answer in
the space next to each item.

To what extent are the following statements true about your company?

Completely False	Mostly False	Somewhat False	Somewhat True	Mostly True	Completely True
0	1	2	3	4	5

1. In this company, people are expected to follow their own
   personal and moral beliefs.
2. People are expected to do anything to further the company's
   interests.
3. In this company, people look out for each other's good.
4. It is very important here to follow strictly the company's rules
   and procedures.
5. In this company, people protect their own interests above
   other considerations.
6. The first consideration is whether a decision violates any law.
7. Everyone is expected to stick by company rules and
   procedures.
8. The most efficient way is always the right way in this
   company.
9. Our major consideration is what is best for everyone in the
   company.
10. In this company, the law or ethical code of the profession is
    the major consideration.
11. It is expected at this company that employees will always do
    what is right for the customer and the public.

Source: B. Victor and J. Cullen, 1988, *Organizational Dynamics*, autumn 1989,
vol. 18, no. 2.

subjective, and benchmarking data will be limited. Whatever
American researchers may want to believe, most managers will
not have thought through the full implications behind the
questions. Overly-simplistic categorisation of organisations as

'caring' or otherwise will need checking against other measures of organisational value-systems before tentative conclusions can be reached.

(b) *Testing the ethical implication of decisions*   Exercises to examine the ethical implications of individual decisions are more specific, and because the analysis is rooted in real case history, may be more relevant and practical.

Alden Lank identifies four simple questions to test ethicality:

- What is the goal underlying the action we are contemplating?
- How do we plan to achieve this goal?
- Deep down, why are we doing this?
- What are the direct and indirect results which we can foresee if we are successful in implementing this decision?[3]

These questions, and their answers, should be at the root of many of the decisions taken by a manager as part of his everyday business activities. Managers should be encouraged to become more self-aware and more analytical in their decision-making, so that they are clear about what factors are influencing them and can understand the wider implications of their decisions.

Laura Nash, in an important *Harvard Business Review* article of 1981, provides a longer list of questions, shown in Table 4.2.

Managers and staff asking themselves questions about the 'rightness' of actions seems a sensible precaution, especially for those engaged in more sensitive purchasing and customer-service functions. The relevance of question 10 in Table 4.2 is clear – a key test is whether you feel comfortable if the action emerges to other people, including, for example, the press. In short, can the action withstand public scrutiny?[4]

(c) *Personal business ethics*   Edgar Wille of the Ashridge Management Research Group drew up a questionnaire of 35 items, an extract of which is shown in Table 4.3.

Table 4.2

Questions to test the ethical implications of a decision

1. Have you defined the problem accurately?
2. How would you define the problem if you stood on the other side of the fence?
3. How did the situation occur in the first place?
4. To whom and to what do you give your loyalty in the first place?
5. What is your intention in making this decision?
6. How does this intention compare with the probable results?
7. Whom could your decision or action injure?
8. Can you discuss the problem with the affected parties before you make your decision?
9. Are you confident that your position will be as valid over a long period as now?
10. Could you disclose without qualm your decision or action to your boss, your chief executive officer, family, society as a whole?
11. What is the symbolic potential of your action if understood? If misunderstood?
12. Under what conditions would you allow exceptions to your stand?

Source: Laura Nash, 'Ethics without the sermon', *Harvard Business Review*, Vol. 59, No. 6, November-December 1981, p. 79–90.

At the beginning of this questionnaire it says 'No one will see this questionnaire but you'. This is clearly vital if such a questionnaire is to be used truthfully.

Ethical guidelines – the questions that arise

From implementing surveys and questionnaires of the type referred to above, the organisation will have a better grasp of the main issues on the ethical agenda, a feel for the dilemmas facing management and staff, and possibly a more general analysis of the climate in the business within which ethical issues are being considered.

Armed with this information, the ethical leader confronts a number of questions:

Table 4.3

Assessing personal business ethics

Personal business ethics			
Do you ever . . .? No one will see this questionnaire but you. Please tick the column nearest the truth.			
	Never	*Sometimes*	*Often*
1. Have you taken stationery or other minor items home from your workplace for personal use?	☐	☐	☐
2. Have you added a little on to your expenses or overtime claims?	☐	☐	☐
3. Have you charged for journeys that cost you nothing, eg train fare when you got a free lift?	☐	☐	☐
4. Have you asked someone to say you're not in when you are?	☐	☐	☐
5. Have you told little lies to clients or customers, eg that something is on order when it's not?	☐	☐	☐
6. Have you shifted the blame for your mistakes to elsewhere in the organisation eg 'It's the computer' or 'Head Office'?	☐	☐	☐
7. Have you used the office phone for personal calls?	☐	☐	☐
8. Have you blamed your subordinates?	☐	☐	☐
9. Have you exaggerated your achievements?	☐	☐	☐
10. Have you minimised the achievement of others?	☐	☐	☐
11. Have you criticised your company to outsiders?	☐	☐	☐
12. Have you criticised senior management to your subordinates?	☐	☐	☐
13. Have you revealed confidential information about people to others?	☐	☐	☐
14. Have you revealed confidential information about your company to others?	☐	☐	☐
15. Have you complained to colleagues about your terms and conditions of service, when you have not taken it up with the appropriate channels?	☐	☐	☐
16. Have you done what you believe to be wrong because everyone else does it?	☐	☐	☐
17. Have you belittled your company's competitors?	☐	☐	☐
18. Have you made false or exaggerated claims about your company?	☐	☐	☐
19. Do you feel deep down, if you are black, that whites are inferior, or, if you are white, that blacks are inferior?	☐	☐	☐
20. If you are a man, do you feel deep down that women are not as a general rule suitable for managerial posts? If you are a woman, do you feel that in general men lack the human understanding necessary for a management post?	☐	☐	☐

Source: Edgar Wille. 'The value of codes of ethics to the individual manager', British Institute of Management Discussion Paper, April 1991, p. 12.

- Should guidelines be issued to managers and staff to assist them in assessing their behaviour in ethical terms?
- What is the form, content and style of guidelines?
- Who is formally responsible for ethics in the organisation?
- How should the guidelines be reinforced and monitored?

These issues will be covered in considerable detail in chapter 7. Each will be briefly discussed here to set the scene for a detailed review of the micro-ethics agenda.

Question 1: Should guidelines be issued?   John Drummond and Bill Bain provide a helpful analysis of the primary advantages and disadvantages of codes of ethics, as shown in Table 4.4.

To the disadvantages we might add that a code can sometimes become an end in itself, rather than a means to an end. 'We have an ethics code, therefore we are an ethical company' would be the tempting conclusion. Yet the vital element in ethical leadership is the ethical behaviour of the managers and staff. The words in a code are less important than the actions that arise day-to-day and how they are dealt with. Cohesive behaviour leads to strength and constancy of purpose. Of course, a code can raise awareness of ethical issues and, as Drummond and Bain state, provide the framework to think through what constitutes acceptable or unacceptable behaviour.

There are other potential problems. Some individuals feel that a code suggests there is an ethical problem, which must be 'solved'. We touched on this when quoting C & J Clark at the beginning of Chapter 1. Others feel a code can be patronising, especially if written in accessible language which can be simplistic, even insulting. Furthermore, to ensure a comprehensive coverage of potential problem areas, codes can become lengthy, complex and prescriptive, serving only as a legal defence later if things go wrong.

Our view is that codes can be helpful. They can provide the opportunity for top management to set the tone over corporate ethics. Managers and staff can better understand that care is

Table 4.4

Advantages and Disadvantages of Codes of Ethics

Reasons for employing ethical codes:

1. To clarify management's thoughts on what constitutes unethical behaviour.
2. To help employees think about ethical issues before they are faced with the realities of the situation.
3. To provide employees with the opportunity of refusing compliance with an unethical action.
4. To define the limits of what constitutes acceptable or unacceptable behaviour.
5. To provide a mechanism for communicating the managerial philosophy in the realm of ethical behaviour.
6. To assist in the induction and training of employees.

Arguments against ethical codes express the following concerns:

1. Even a detailed list of guidelines cannot be expected to cover all the possible grey areas of potentially unethical practices.
2. Like fair-employment practice statements, codes of ethics are often too generalised to be of specific value.
3. Rarely are codes of ethics prioritised; for example, loyalty to the company and to fellow employees does not resolve the potential conflict when a colleague is seen to be acting contrary to company interests.
4. As an individual phenomenon, ethical behaviour which has been guided by ethical codes of conduct will only be effective if the codes have been internalised and are truly believed by employees.

Source: John Drummond and Bill Bain, *Managing Business Ethics*, Oxford, Butterworth-Heinemann, 1994, p. 204.

needed over *how* results are obtained, not just that they *are* obtained. As we have already noted, the long-term reputation and integrity of the organisation are precious, and great importance should be attached to preserving such reputational assets.

A code must not be constructed in such a way that it defines certain behaviour as black or white, right or wrong. It should not be perceived as a collection of company rules. If it is to be used it must be seen as a living document, and if necessary a changing document, seen as providing support to employees who are faced with grey areas, where different outcomes can have varying advantages and disadvantages. The code can help them to assess the relative strengths of the different outcomes.

Consideration will also need to be given to the title of the code . The word 'ethics' can be off-putting. The phrase 'Code of Business Conduct' is more appropriate. The British Airways title: 'The way we do things. . . the code of business conduct' gives the subject an accessible feel.

Question 2: The form, content and style of guidelines   One study of corporate codes of ethics in UK businesses concluded that three basic formats could be distinguished:

(1) Regulatory documents with detailed rules and guide-lines, giving staff precise advice on behaviour and conduct (eg Mobil Holdings, Albright & Wilson, Petrofina, and British Gas).
(2) Shorter, more generally-phrased codes providing statements about the company's aims, objectives, philosophy or values, which exclude specific guidance on employee behaviour (e.g. Sainsburys, British Tele-com, DRG, and ICL).
(3) Elaborate codes covering a wide range of topics, including an outline of the company's social responsi-bilities to a wide range of stakeholders (eg Boots, Shell, Coats Viyella, Reckitt & Colman, Ciba-Geigy, and Esso UK).[5]

Much depends on what the objectives of the code are. Gerald Vinton defines three types of code: the regulatory code, the aspirational code, and the educational code. The regulatory code contains imperatives which are so compelling as to require no further discussion. The aspirational code provides a standard to aspire to, and the educational code aims for enlightened discussion of the issues.[6]

Studying codes written either in the USA or in Britain, it can be seen that US codes are often more elaborate, more legal/regulatory and prescriptive. British examples tend to be more aspirational or educational, with greater emphasis on the vision and values of the organisation. This sets the ethical tone within which individuals judge their responses rather than providing detailed information on precise actions. This difference may be at least partly explained by the different legal context in the USA referred to in Chapter 2.

Another issue which is relevant to multi-national or multi-business organisations is whether the code should be universal covering all segments of the business or tailored to the specific requirements of each individual unit. The problems here are well known. The more corporate the code is, the more general it might have to become. Even worse, managers and staff in the different regions/business units may not own it, or identify with it. Lack of effective ownership or feelings of accountability can result in the document (beautifully produced though it may be) remaining firmly on the shelf.

Each organisation has to think through this area for itself. We prefer a base document of key elements of the organisation's vision, values and ethical principles with individual regions/businesses taking responsibility for adding specific elements relevant to their position.

Question 3: Who is responsible?   Despite the wide range of books and articles on the subject of business ethics, little assistance is given on who in the organisation should be responsible for producing and monitoring the code of business conduct. Overall, of course, the chairman or chief executive officer is likely to be responsible for the ethics of the corporation;[7] and line management must take responsibility for day-to-day actions. Within those general assertions, there are many options for specific functional accountability including:

- company secretary's department
- internal audit
- personnel
- corporate affairs.

The Company Secretary, with analogous responsibilities for

corporate governance and shareholder services, can be relevant especially if this function also includes legal accountabilities. This, however, may give the subject a more legal/regulatory dimension. A similar problem might exist with internal audit. Personnel might be perceived – we tread delicately here, given our publisher – as more remote from the business issues although, ironically, this may be an advantage, suggesting impartiality! Corporate affairs may be too much identified with PR and therefore with positioning the business to best advantage. This can produce a more cynical reaction internally and externally than is desirable.

We can make no firm recommendation. Each organisation will differ in the way it allocates responsibilities, and therefore each organisation must think the position through very carefully. It is vital that line managers retain overall ownership and that no central function detracts from this clear accountability. We return to the overall role of HR in ethics in chapter 8.

Question 4: Reinforcing and monitoring guidelines Codes of business conduct cannot just be launched into the organisation. Careful consultation with employees at all levels will be necessary. Once a code is designed in this participative manner, it can be reinforced in many different ways including:

- training – using real case-studies from the organisation
- linking ethical issues to performance objectives within a performance management culture
- using the disciplinary procedure for proven breaches of the code
- insisting all staff sign for a copy of the code, and any update
- including reference to the code in recruitment and induction
- referring to ethical behaviour in company communication videos and other forms of information
- forming an ethics committee to monitor criteria
- appointing an ethics officer and ethics counsellors
- developing and publicising a whistle-blowing procedure.
- issuing codes of practice for all consultants and agents acting

on behalf of the company – and reinforcing this in the terms
of engagement and in training
• conducting audits and surveys of ethical actions (similar to
those described above).

We return in detail to these reinforcing mechanisms in
Chapters 6 and 7.

The micro-ethics agenda

Having briefly examined these preliminary questions, we now
need to review some of the micro-ethics issues on the agenda.
The reader will recall our definition of micro-ethics: those day-
to-day issues which raise ethical concerns which most managers
will face in the workplace.
  Bearing this definition in mind, we will explore four areas:

• receiving and giving of gifts and hospitality
• personal conflicts of interest
• confidentiality
• relationship with suppliers.

We start with the sensitive issue of receiving and giving gifts
and hospitality.

Gifts and hospitality   The giving and receiving of gifts and
hospitality has been an accepted part of business practice for a
long time. The level of such gifts and hospitality is often
determined by past and present practices in the particular
industry the company is in, and can vary greatly from industry
to industry and from country to country. Trends come and go,
of course, and the growing awareness of ethical implications
coupled with a greater emphasis on leanness has led to an
overall diminution in recent years amongst many companies.

However, no organisation will want to be seen as trying to gain improper advantage by offering anything that could be construed as a bribe. As one company put it:

> The company's business interests are best served when its relationships are based on commercial criteria and not influenced by such factors as gifts or entertainment.

Similarly, no organisation will want to be placed in a position of being obligated to people who offer gifts or hospitality.

So far, so good. However, networking is a valuable – indeed vital – element of corporate effectiveness. Maintaining and enhancing successful business relationships will involve meetings, and sometimes entertainment will be involved.

Most organisations recognise that hospitality cannot be prohibited, and in these circumstances the emphasis turns to ensuring that the entertainment is infrequent and of moderate value. Critically, there has to be an understanding that a definite business purpose is being served. This test has to be applied each time this issue arises.

A good example of how this matter is treated in a Code of Business Conduct can be seen in Table 4.5.

On gifts, some organisations adopt a categorical 'no gifts' policy which leaves employees with no discretion. Gifts received are returned – politely – and great sensitivity will be necessary in doing this in some parts of the world. Alternatively, a gift may be declared – perhaps in a 'bung book' – and then donated to a charity of the giver's choice, or if it is modest, kept by the recipient.

Some organisations define what is meant by 'modest' – figures of up to £15 or £20 are typical. This generally allows seasonal gifts to be retained.

Another useful and well-judged example of such a policy is that of the Burton Group from their Code of Business Conduct shown in Table 4.6.

Gifts and entertainment within the company also needs careful consideration to avoid any misunderstandings.

Table 4.5
Entertainment outside the company

Entertainment outside the Company	
Entertaining includes dining, drinking, attending an amusement or cultural event, or participating in a recreational or related activity.	Employees should not give or receive extravagant entertainment, including free airline tickets, hotel accommodation that is not strictly necessary for business purposes, or free use of expensive recreational facilities.
Employees may give or receive entertainment on infrequent occasions of moderate value on the understanding that a definite business purpose is being served. Such entertainment should be appropriate to the business and responsibilities of the individual and be capable of reciprocation as a normal business expense.	Home entertainment for the Company's account should be cleared in advance (including the guest list) by an employee's department head. A complete record of the cost of entertaining, including receipts, should be submitted on the appropriate expense account forms.

Source: Esso plc, *Standards of Business Conduct*, p. 18 – quoted with permission.

Personal conflicts of interest A fairly common micro-ethics issue for the ethical leader to consider is in situations where personal or family interests may conflict with the interests of the group.

Any financial interest in a competitor or supplier may cause difficulties and be perceived as divided loyalties. Outside employment – as MPs will testify – can raise concerns, too, as can insider-trading.

Table 4.7 shows the form of words adopted by United Biscuits on the issue of Conflicts of Interest.

Some organisations have developed conflicts of interest questionnaires which are sent to all staff, and regularly updated. Extracts from such a questionnaire are shown at Table 4.8.

As many codes point out, 'your private life is your own'. However, in considering micro-ethics managers and staff have a responsibility to avoid situations in which loyalty may become

Table 4.6
Dealing with gifts in Burton Group

To avoid any possibility of bias or compromise, the following rules apply:

a) Employees must never accept personal payment, gift or reward (in any form whatsoever) in the course of their dealings with external suppliers.

Incentives such as competition prizes may be accepted provided such schemes are approved in advance by the appropriate personnel and retail operations directors. All such incentive schemes must be co-ordinated by personnel/retail operations to ensure their proper operation, tax treatment and that the result is incremental business rather than a shift between brands/ranges.

b) Christmas gifts of nominal value such as a pocket diary or a bottle of wine may be accepted from suppliers.

Nominal value will never include anything with a retail value in excess of £20. Excepted from this policy are gifts from a supplier to an entire buying team or department. These can be accepted provided they are not kept by any employee for personal use but are distributed within a department as directed by the divisional director (eg a box of chocolates).

Any gifts which do not fall under the categories defined above may not be accepted by any employee of the Group and they must be returned to the donor with a note explaining that the gift may not be accepted because it is in violation of Burton Group policy.

c) The above notwithstanding, it is also the policy of the Group that no employees may accept any gift at any location other than at their place of work, unless it is received in connection with an approved incentive scheme noted in a) above.

d) Employees must never accept holidays paid for by suppliers. Any working trips paid for by suppliers must have the *prior written* authorisation of the appropriate divisional Managing Director or equivalent.

Source: Burton Group, *Code of Business Conduct*, p. 2 – quoted with permission.

divided. This applies, too, to situations where an employee's spouse may work for a competitor or supplier.

IBM in their Code of Business Conduct, handle this matter most tactfully, as shown in Table 4.9.

Table 4.7

Ethics and conflicts of interest

Conflicts of Interest

Public Issues
An employee will avoid conflict of interest by making it known that he or she is employed by UB and that views expressed on public, political or civic affairs are those of the individual and not necessarily of the company.

Financial Interests
No director or senior manager or other employee with privileged or financially sensitive 'inside' information may deal in the company's shares without first notifying the directors in writing of their intention and receiving a written acknowledgement of that notification. No employee may make known to any person outside the company material information about the company's operations or performance which could influence share dealing.

No employee should have any financial interest in a competitor or supplier which could cause divided loyalty or even the appearance of divided loyalty. Nor should an employee have any other financial interest which could cause speculation or misunderstanding about why he or she has that interest.

Activity for Personal Gain
No employee may be involved with activity for personal gain which for any reason is in conflict with UB's business interests, nor may work be solicited or performed which could be in competition with UB. Unless authorised by a director, no outside work may be performed or business or clients be solicited in company time or on company premises. Nor may company owned equipment, materials, resources or inside information be used for outside work without similar authorisation.

Source: United Biscuits, quoted in Simon Webley, *Business Ethics and Company Codes*, Institute of Business Ethics, 1992, p. 24.

Confidentiality All organisations are provided with information from customers, suppliers and employees, about themselves and their businesses. They expect such information to be kept confidential and for it not be misused. Similarly, information which is confidential about the company should not be revealed externally without prior agreement of senior management.

Table 4.8

Typical Conflict of Interest questionnaire

Direct and indirect interests and interests in common

Identify all interests (including passive investments) which you, your spouse or any members of your family have had in the last eighteen months:

(a) in any business with which the company, or any subsidiary of the company, has done business

(b) in any business in which any present or former employee, agent, or director of the company, or any subsidiary of the company, has had any interest (including passive investments).

Table 4.9

IBM's Code of Business Conduct*

Someone Close to You Working in the Industry

With the growth in two-career families and the expansion of the industry, you may find yourself in a situation where your spouse, another member of your immediate family, or someone else you are close to is a competitor or supplier of IBM or is employed by one.

While everyone is entitled to choose and pursue a career, such situations call for extra sensitivity to security, confidentiality and conflicts of interest. The closeness of the relationship might lead you inadvertently to compromise IBM's interests.

There are several factors to consider in assessing such a situation. Among them are the relationship between IBM and the other company; the nature of your responsibilities as an IBM employee and those of the person close to you; and the access each of you has to your respective employer's confidential information.

You should also be aware that the situation, however harmless it may appear to you, could arouse suspicions among your associates that might affect your working relationships. The very appearance of a conflict of interest can create problems, regardless of the behaviour of the IBM employee involved.

To remove any such doubts or suspicions, you should review your specific situation with your manager to assess the nature and extent of any concern and how it can be resolved. Frequently, any risk to IBM's interests is sufficiently remote that your manager need only remind you of such matters as guarding against inadvertently disclosing IBM confidential information. However, in some instances, a change in the job responsibilities of one of the people involved may be necessary.

* (Quoted with permission.)

An example of the treatment of this micro-ethics issue, from United Biscuits, is shown in Table 4.10.

Table 4.10
Confidentiality procedures in United Biscuits

Confidentiality
Confidential information about our business is the property of the company. Only those people with a business 'need to know' should have access to confidential information and such information may not be disclosed to anyone within or outside the company without the authority of a director.
Information about customers or suppliers, or indeed about any organisation or individual, must not be misused.
Personal information about employees must only be collected, used and retained where it is required for business or legal reasons and will only be available to those with a clear business 'need to know'. Any decision on use of personal information for valid business purposes will be weighed against the individual's right to privacy.
The company's health care specialists are employed as impartial advisors and their actions are governed at all times by their professional codes of ethics. Access to clinical data is confined to the occupational physicians and nurses and no confidential information may be disclosed to any others without the consent of the individual employee.

Source: Simon Webley, *Business Ethics and Company Codes*, Institute of Business Ethics, 1992, p. 24.

Areas for the ethical leader to specifically consider in relation to confidentiality include:

- security arrangements
- all customer records
- personnel and medical records
- business and marketing plans
- research and development proposals

- financial data, including details of profitability, dividends, and gearing
- details of future company plans, including acquisitions, disposals, and restructurings
- sources of supply of 'own brand' products
- special promotions

Computer security is relevant here. As one company code put it:

> The company's policy on computer security requires all employees to act responsibly when dealing with the storage, access and use of computerised data. Employees have a duty to protect assets and information from improper access or use by others.

Relationship with suppliers Ethical issues in relation to suppliers covers, in part, the subjects already referred to above, including receiving payments or gifts from existing or potential suppliers. There are two separate themes here: how the company deals with its suppliers in an ethical manner, and the ethical standards the company expects of its suppliers.

In Chapter 2, we identified some of the problems in relation to suppliers, including paying on time, and ensuring standards of quality are achieved. These can be translated to ethical principles such as:

- Suppliers and sub-contractors will be paid on time and in accordance with agreed terms of trade.
- Suppliers and sub-contractors will be provided with all relevant information so that they can effectively contribute to quality objectives.
- The person who employs the supplier or sub-contractor will not be the same person who agrees how much they are paid or other contract terms.

The well thought-through example of Welsh Water shown in

Table 4.11 also raises the issue of the responsibility of the
company to small firms.

Table 4.11

*Relationship with suppliers in Welsh Water's Statement
of Corporate Ethics**

As a major purchaser of goods and services the company accepts the need to behave responsibly and with integrity in its dealings with all suppliers, both in the UK and overseas. Agreements made with suppliers will be specified carefully and accurately to avoid future misunderstanding, and any agreements made will be met fully and promptly. All suppliers or potential suppliers will be given a fair opportunity to offer their goods or services to the company.
Many of the company's suppliers will be small firms and the company fully recognises its wider responsibilities to such firms. The company is aware that through its dealings with suppliers it is often in a position to influence the economic stability and viability of smaller firms. It will not take any unreasonable advantage of its trading position in such circumstances but will ensure that suppliers are treated in a fair and equitable manner.
Relationships and agreements with suppliers will always be based upon normal commercial considerations and the giving or taking of hospitality between individual employees and representatives of the supplier will be conducted according to strict standards of ethical behaviour and company policy.
In making any agreement with a supplier, Welsh Water plc will take into consideration the extent to which the supplier's policies and procedures conform to the company's code of ethics.

* (Quoted with permission).

Summary

Following consideration of the 'big picture' issues of vision and
ethics in Chapter 3, this chapter has described approaches to
identifying micro-ethical issues in the workplace. This included
ethical climate questionnaires and specific questions aimed at

testing the ethical implications of a decision. Having established the ethical agenda, a number of questions were discussed, including: should guidelines be issued to all managers and staff on ethical concerns and who should be responsible for ethics in the organisation?

Subsequently, four examples of the micro-ethics agenda were explored in detail: gifts and hospitality, conflicts of interest, confidentiality, and dealing with suppliers. Examples of company codes of conduct were included to illustrate in practical terms how guidelines might be shaped in these areas.

In the final analysis, micro-ethical issues can be evaluated by asking certain straightforward questions: Is it right? Is it fair? Can I disclose it? Unethical behaviour, when it occurs, is generally understood as such by the individual. The guidelines described in this chapter will, it is hoped, assist managers and staff to make the right judgements.

References

1. John B. Cullen, Bart Victor, Carroll Stephens, 'An ethical weather report: assessing the organisation's ethical climate', *Organisational Dynamics*, Autumn 1989, pp. 59–60.
2. Alan Weiss, 'Seven reasons to examine workplace ethics', *HR Magazine*, March 1991, p. 72.
3. Alden G. Lank, 'Building the ethical corporation: luxury or necessity', *European Business Journal*, 2/3, 1990, p. 54.
4. For more information on ethics checklists see Michael R. Hyman, Robert Skipper and Richard Tansey, 'Ethical Codes are not enough', *Business Horizons*, March–April 1990, pp. 17–21.
5. Bodo B. Schleselmilch and Jane E. Houston 'Corporate codes of ethics', *Management Decision*, 28, 7, 1990, pp. 40–41.
6. For more details on these definitions, see Gerald Vinton, 'Business ethics: busy body or corporate conscience?' *Leadership and Organisation Development Journal*, 11, 3, 1992, pp. 10–11.
7. This was confirmed in one study in 1991; see Simon Webley *Business Ethics and Company Codes*, Institute of Business Ethics, 1992, p. 22.

5

◼◼ Tackling Ethics through
Values

Both macro-ethical and micro-ethical issues are informed by underlying values. We have already demonstrated the significant links between vision and ethics (in Chapter 3); we now go on to examine the crucial significance of explicit values for the ethical leader and the ethical organisation. Looking first at the detailed reasons why values are important, we explore the factors which influence organisational values and the relationship between ethical values on the one hand and ethical behaviour on the other. Especially important, from the ethical leader's standpoint, is the impact of the organisation's ethical values on its reputation, and therefore on its competitive position.

Why values are important

In Chapter 3's discussion on vision and ethics, we argued firmly that every organisation has values of some sort, even if they are purely opportunistic and instrumental, and even if the values are never consciously articulated. Individuals within organisations, too, have their own values and therefore their own ethical standpoints. In most cases these values will be distinct from, and in some instances very different from, the ethical posture of the organisation.

Publishing a set of declared corporate values is an attempt to specify business-conduct guidelines that, as a minimum, will constrain and direct the actions of the employees in their corporate roles. Such a set of ethical values – accompanied by a derived code of conduct – can change the culture for the better, helping to influence the ethical beliefs of the employees towards an internally coherent and externally visible framework of assumptions, attitudes, behaviour, and caveats.

In our view, declared ethical values serve several purposes:

- They supply both prescriptive and proscriptive parameters for ethical behaviour.
- They are helpful in attracting suitable employees and in deterring others.
- They generate mutual confidence among suppliers, customers and shareholders.

Ethical leadership is seldom built exclusively around materialistic goals like increased profitability. However, ethical values do have commercial relevance:

- Our discussion of shareholder priorities, in Chapter 2, reinforced the point that investors may take their funds elsewhere if the corporate values seem to distract attention away from a capital/dividend growth focus. It is important, therefore, that the declared values have a strongly commercial thrust.
- The ethical values of the organisation have to be aligned to the expectations of customers – otherwise the customers will go elsewhere. Two examples: Gerald Ratner's dismissive comments about his company's products and, by implication, his contemptuous view of Ratner's customers; and Turner & Newall's handling of the increased concern about the hazardous effects of blue asbestos.
- Increasingly, customers are interested in the values displayed by the companies with which they do business. They expect organisations to have clearly expressed values which have resonance with their own priority concerns, and will take their custom to such organisations. Examples include Marks & Spencer, Bodyshop, and the Co-operative Bank. In Chapter 3 we referred to these organisations as having 'aspirational' visions.
- Declared values may become a valuable means of generating

both employee and supplier commitment, hence promoting superior performance at both the 'input' and 'output' ends of the 'value-added' equation. Instances supporting this argument embrace the John Lewis Partnership, Remploy, and many organisations in the public or third (not-for-profit) sectors like local government and charities.

In 1976 IBM proclaimed its belief that every company should have a code of conduct that clearly spells out the legal and ethical obligations of corporate leadership, as one of the best ways to assure the survival of business in the future. From the vantage-point of the 1990s it is clear that many well-managed organisations understand the crucial significance of value statements as an ingredient in their profitability and in their strategic orientation.

The SmithKline Beecham 'Simply Better' core values illustrate how values can shape an organisation's strategic programmes. The five values are summarised in Table 5.1.

Table 5.1
SmithKline Beecham: The Five Core Values

---

1 **Performance**: 'SB is performance-driven. We aim to continuously improve performance in all that we do.'
2 **Customers**: 'SB is customer-orientated. We strive to provide products and services of superior value to meet the expectations of our internal and external customers.'
3 **Innovation**:'SB constantly strives to be creative and innovative on all its endeavours. All SB employees and encouraged to bring forth new and better ideas for improved performance, whatever their responsibilities.'
4 **People**: 'SB employees are all partners, working together in the pursuit of the SB mission and strategy. We strongly value teamwork, and want every employee to be motivated to succeed.'
5 **Integrity**:'SB demands openness and honesty throughout its operations to engender trust, and integrity underscores everything that we do. We believe that every activity must be able to pass the test of public and internal scrutiny at all times.'

Source: SmithKline Beecham Corporate Affairs Department (reproduced with permission).

The SmithKline Beecham values, as we pointed out in Chapter 1, are an example of transcendental ethics in action, as the company has sought to apply these same values – and the derived nine 'leadership practices', not reprinted here – across its entire global network, with only minimal concessions to local conditions. The same is true for the five values reflected in what Philips Electronics – another global company – calls 'The Philips Way' (see Table 5.2).

In essence, we believe that explicit values, like those produced for Philips and SmithKline Beecham, are important, for 10 good reasons.

1 *They supply behavioural and decisional frameworks for the organisation's managers.* As organisations grow, it is no longer sufficient to rely on the chief executive to be the sole guardian, protector and promoter of the company's ethical stance. Both the SmithKline Beecham five values and The Philips Way are especially relevant to global, diversified organisations whose CEOs cannot be everywhere at once.

2 *They define action parameters for new employees and promote an ethical culture which becomes a way of life for the workforce across the board.* Younger employees in particular are likely to have received little or no 'training' in ethical behaviour. Not only do they need clear guidelines, but the organisation has to generate such guidelines in order to prevent misunderstandings about what is acceptable and unacceptable behaviour. Conduct based on short-term profit maximisation, without regard to any other ethical dimension, can be ruinous for the enterprise. In Chapter 2 we referred to Gellerman's explanation about the circumstances in which otherwise 'good' managers can make 'bad' ethical choices: one of these scenarios occurs when employees believe themselves to be acting in accordance with the requirements of the organisation when in fact their view of the organisation's 'best interests' is, at best, misguided. The case of Virgin Atlantic's treatment at the hands of some free-spirit British Airways

Table 5.2
Philips Electronics: The Philips Way

---

1 Delight customers
- Listen to customers and actively seek their opinion.
- Add value through all your actions – ask yourself, 'Am I actively improving Philips products or services through this action?'
- Make the customer visible, especially to those not in day-to-day contact with customers.
- Be a business partner, not simply a supplier – look at all your actions from the customer's point of view.
- Treat both internal and external suppliers as a valued part of the customer's supply chain.

2 Value people as our greatest resource
- Ensure every employee has equal opportunity for recognition and career development.
- Monitor, coach and support people – look for opportunities to encourage personal development, and act on them.
- Listen and communicate to all levels – make time to hear views and give out information.
- Be willing and able to reward fairly – define how we expect others to behave and what we want them to achieve, and make sure we are consistent in our rewards.

3 Deliver quality and excellence in all actions
- Understand quality, ask yourself 'How can I deliver quality in my own role and encourage others to do the same?'
- Demonstrate commitment to quality – let others see us delivering quality, show them how to follow suit, and reward achievements.

4 Achieve premium return on equity
- Set clear financial targets and make sure your colleagues understand them and know how to achieve them.
- Commit to these targets – do not move the goalposts.
- Maintain continuous cost evaluation – and educate others to do the same.
- Make our financial targets your number one priority.

5 Encourage entrepreneurial behaviour at all levels
- Encourage freedom of ideas within clearly defined borders – educate your colleagues to understand what makes an idea a truly practical suggestion.
- Use realistic reporting – work on an idea before submitting it and encourage others to do the same.
- Agree risk assessment – look at the risks and present the pros and cons formally, in writing.
- Be a supporter – you are part of the team, so support with actions, not just words.
- Select, reward and promote people who demonstrate entrepreneurial behaviour.

Source: Philips Electronics (UK) Limited (reproduced with permission).

executives shows that even when employee motives are well-intentioned, the adverse consequences can be significant – always a potential difficulty when relying excessively on the kind of social ethics which we described in Chapter 1 as little more than a sophisticated version of group loyalty.

3 *Values underpin the strategic direction of the organisation.*
If vision and ethics have to be in alignment (as we argued in Chapter 3) with the corporate strategy, then the organisation's values must be similarly positioned. In one typical company investigated for purposes of this book, it was made clear to us by the chairman that the firm's 'statement of values' was consistent with the vision and the strategic plan: all three focused on the company's customers and the superior service which had to be supplied if the organisation was to remain differentiated from its competitors. Where strategy and values are not consistent, the result will be corporate confusion. Sometimes an organisation will have values but no strategy. This occurs in some local authorities and third-sector (not-for-profit) organisations, where a kind of latent strategy emerges through individual managers each translating their 'service' or 'altruistic' beliefs into spontaneous action.

4 *Values convey expectations about the conduct of the organisation's stakeholders.* By encouraging a high standard of behaviour among employees, companies signal to their shareholders, their suppliers, and their customers the fact that they categorically reject illegal or improper business activity. When a third party suggests something questionable, more-over, managers or other employees can use the values as an impersonal defence in order to justify rejection of whatever is being proposed.

5 *Publication of core values will enhance the company's public image and raise levels of customer confidence.* Once a strong ethical 'credit balance' has been secured, the organisation benefits from its reputational assets. Any transgression is

likely to be perceived as a one-off accident, and will be forgiven.

6 *Values reduce and pre-empt the possibility of legal action.* Corporate values, especially when bolstered by an organisational code of conduct, will contribute to the avoidance of aggressive litigation. Not only can the presence of such values be cited for defensive purposes, and as a justification for disowning 'cowboy' employees, but the values themselves will reduce the likelihood of questionable activities occurring in the first place.

7 *Values benefit the bottom-line results.* Statements of corporate values raise the important question of how values relate to profits. As Quigley[1] points out, 'It is critically important to see values and profits in their proper perspective, as partners and not opponents. *Profit* is viewed with disdain by many who fail to understand its role in the economy at large and as a reward to the superior performer . . . Values are the primary drivers or motivators and profit the reward.' In the USA, the Ethics Resource Center examined 21 American companies which maintain codes of conduct. If a person had invested $30,000 in the Dow Jones Industrial Average Index, it would have been worth $134,000 three decades later; however, the return from investing the same sum in those 21 companies would have been almost nine times greater.[2]

In addition, the financial benefits from producing explicit corporate values are multi-faceted. Sales opportunities as well as employee productivity can improve. Employees do not waste time in speculating about the degree to which they can seek advantage from unethical or questionable behaviour. Further, the ethical values of the organisation can be a powerful source of sustainable competitive advantage, particularly where the wording contains a strong customer focus. This is the way in which the US chainstore group, Nordstrom, welcomes its new staff:

We're glad to have you with our Company. Our number

one goal is to provide *outstanding customer service*. Set both your personal and professional goals high. We have great confidence in your ability to achieve them. Nordstrom Rules: Rule No 1: *Use your good judgment in all situations*. There will be no additional rules. Please feel free to ask your department manager, store manager, or divisional general manager any question at any time.[3]

8 *Values are a powerful mechanism for integrating merged or acquired organisations.* Once employees become familiar with the surviving or parent organisation's ethical and business conduct guidelines – and are persuaded to take them seriously – then they can be speedily assimilated into the new structure, or may elect to transfer their talent elsewhere. Cultural and operational fusion is especially important in growing organisations and because large size is normally linked to a reduced sense of responsibility among individual employees.

9 *Values deter managers from issuing improper instructions to staff – and also deter staff from making improper approaches to managers.* The vast majority of corporate codes and ethical value statements will make it clear that no one at any level in the organisation has authority to require or request people to behave in a manner contrary to the values and the code.

10 *Values encourage open communications.* It is common for direct and honest communication to be presented as a key value in itself, as we have seen from the SmithKline Beecham and Philips Electronics examples. Direct and honest communications, once established, have obvious benefits over a situation where views are suppressed, disagreement is interpreted as disloyalty, and ideas remain stillborn.

In Chapter 3 we spoke out strongly about the benefits to be gained from a clear-cut, coherent vision for any organisation. In turn, values and beliefs are the most fundamental of the elements within a corporate vision. Values precede vision and goals in both logic and reality. In 1977, five years prior to their publication of *In Search of Excellence*, Peters and Waterman wrote about the significance of 'superordinate goals', which they describe as 'a set of values and aspirations, often unwritten, that goes beyond the conventional formal statement of corporate objectives. Superordinate goals are the fundamental ideas around which a business is built. They are its main values.'[4] Subsequently, McKinsey made 'superordinate goals' part of its 'Seven S' framework, the crucial elements of all corporations. To be meaningful, values, vision, and ethics need to be spelt out.

For instance, we could speculate on the dilemmas faced by an organisation which has some declared values, but which has not bothered to produce a vision statement. Thus we would know how people are expected to behave, but not what they are expected to accomplish. To use the language of group dynamics, they would be more concerned about *process* than about *outcomes*. Companies like People Express, once regarded as 'excellent' in the Peters and Waterman lexicon, fell for precisely this reason. Their obsession with implementing neo-humanistic values internally took precedence over marketplace responsiveness. This is a significant contemporary issue for some of the Christian Churches, in our view.

Should vision and values fail to be integrated, then employees must confront intolerable difficulties when making strategic, tactical or operational choices. What they will do to make their ambiguity tolerable is to ignore all published pronouncements about vision and ethical values, but to pay assiduous attention to what senior management actually does: what they say, how they apportion priorities, what actions are rewarded, what initiatives are welcomed, ignored or punished, how power is exercised, and so forth. This is not ethical leadership, nor ethical 'followership'. It is life dictated by short-term expediency, a Darwinian struggle for survival, and the shifting sands of political games diverting attention away from the strategic ball.

The links between values and ethics

Values inspire ethical beliefs; ethical beliefs influence attitudes; attitudes underpin behaviour. Behaviour – what people do – is what matters for organisations, but behaviour is only the tip of an iceberg composed variously of ethical values, ethical principles, attitudes, and all sorts of psychological or philosophical assumptions which we carry round with us as a kind of psychic baggage.

In an ideal world, values, beliefs, attitudes, and behaviour will propel people in the same direction. Unfortunately, the world is not ideal. It is possible for attitudes and values on the one hand, and actions and behaviour on the other, to generate oppositional tensions. Cabin crew members in a commercial airline may transmit all the correct and professional signals – body language, eye contact, smiles, considerate and helpful phrases – while simultaneously hating the work they do and despising the passengers. This role-conflict can be sustained for a long time, especially if the rewards outweigh the penalties, but the psychological price is high. From a managerial viewpoint it would be preferable if the personality characteristics of the in-flight staff were positively aligned towards people, and specifically towards the fare-paying customers.

At a corporate level, differences between the declared corporate values and the actions of senior managers and much harder to conceal. If an organisation is to adopt a high-profile set of ethical values, and expects senior executives to behave in accordance with these principles, then work has to be done to ensure that the ethical values are internalised rather than merely 'painted on' so that they can be as easily peeled off again. Some techniques and tools for achieving internal commitment to a corporate framework of ethical values are examined in Chapter 6.

In Chapter 4 we cited Vinton in support of the view that there are three types of ethical code commonly generated by organisations:

- *Regulatory* – containing imperatives which have to be sustained, if only for compliance purposes;
- *Aspirational* – reflecting a goal to be attained;
- *Educational* – aiming at enlightened discussion of the issues so that standards improve through reflective enlightenment.[5]

Somewhat similarly, ethical values may be *descriptive* (portraying what is already the case) or *normative* (suggesting what ought to be the case). The former, if taken at face value, suggests no requirement for behaviour change apart from those individuals who have not yet seen the light. The latter – reflected in the accompaniment to the five values of The Philips Way – represents a series of goals towards which recruitment/selection, motivation/leadership, training/development, and performance/improvement criteria will be coaxed and cajoled.

A clear example of the descriptive mode of thinking is expressed within Ericsson's 'Our Values' statement (Table 5.3).[6]

Table 5.3
Ericsson: 'Our Values'

Operations
Ericsson is an international company and we focus on its totality when performing our tasks and satisfying customers' needs
Customers
A customer is a partner in co-operation with whom we establish long-term customer relations
The individual
We stimulate the creation of an open, straightforward and instructive working climate
Leadership
Our leaders inspire us with team-spirit and create positive relations
Organisation
Our organisation allows profit responsibility to be decentralised in operations managed by objectives

Source: Midi Berry and William Keyser in Ralph Stacey (ed.) *Strategic Thinking and the Management of Change*, p. 156.[3]

Another instance of the descriptive approach is the list of ethical values produced by Herman Miller Inc. Notably, these were not defined explicitly as part of a reaction to external stress, but were generated proactively in order to express the distinctiveness of the Herman Miller organisation.

Table 5.4

Herman Miller Inc: Innovation and Excellence through Participative Ownership

- **Innovation**: We seek and encourage appropriate problem-solving designs and innovative solutions that deliver results for our customers and meet our business challenges.
- **Excellence**: We create value for our customers by providing quality and excellence in all that we do and the way in which we do it.
- **Participation**: We work together in teams, with each person contributing to the level of his or her capabilities.
- **Ownership**: We each have a stake in the organisation in which we invest our lives and share the risks and rewards of ownership.
- **Leadership**: We can lead best by enabling others and by being dedicated to achieving our corporate vision.

Source: Statement of Corporate Values of Herman Miller Inc, cited in Joseph V. Quigley, *Vision: How Leaders Develop It, Share It, and Sustain It*. New York, McGraw Hill, 1993, p. 20.

A normative set of ethical values is the 'Aspirations Statement' from Levi's, reproduced below in Table 5.5.

Descriptive and normative value statements each carry risks. If an organisation describes what it believes to be currently the case, and its actions are perceived to be different, it is open to the charge of hypocrisy. The people who drew up the allegedly 'descriptive' statement will be seen as dangerously out of touch with reality. The outcome is a recipe for cynicism among the organisation's stakeholders.

If the organisation talks about what should be, and acknowledges that it is not there yet, the new age may never dawn because the obstacles which currently prevent people from

Table 5.5
The Levi's 'Aspirations' Statement

We all want a company that our people are proud of and committed to, where all employees have an opportunity to contribute, learn, grow, and advance based on merit, not politics or background. We want out people to feel respected, treated fairly, listened to, and involved. Above all, we want satisfaction from accomplishments and friendships, balanced personal and professional lives, and to have fun in our endeavours.

When we describe the kind of Levi Strauss & Co we want in the future, what we are talking about is building on the foundation we have inherited: affirming the best of our company's traditions, closing gaps that may exist between principles and practices, and updating some of our values to reflect contemporary circumstances.

Source: Midi Berry and William Keyser, pp. 156–157.[3]

behaving as they should will continue to manifest themselves ('I will be good but, please God, not yet').

Developing ethical values in an organisation

Politicians are often keen to reify 'society'. For similar reasons, CEOs typically seek to promote 'the company' as the object of loyalty and commitment. Corporate advertising (eg BP, Hanson) promotes this focus and distracts attention from what can seem to be an unhealthy reliance on the charisma of a powerful leader (Akio Morita, Robert Maxwell, Alan Sugar).

The drive for ethical values accentuates this depersonalisation process. Values encourage continuity ('The King is dead, long live the ethical values') and supply a constraining influence over the actions of corporate management. Nonetheless, decisions are made by individuals, not by organisations. This being so, the emergence of ethical values is likely to be inspired by a specific ethical leader, rather than spring spontaneously from the inbuilt momentum of corporate progress.

We believe there are broadly three types of cultural paradigm so far as the development of explicit ethical values are concerned: profit-focused, customer-focused or people-focused.

In the *profit-focused* structure, the dominant orientation of the key players is materialistic. Managers are unlikely to initiate or take kindly to a published statement of ethical values. On the other hand, they will often have elaborate rules related to such matters as the giving and receiving of gifts and Christmas gratuities, and, if they are companies in the financial services sector, they will be subject to detailed compliance systems. So, for the profit-focused organisation, if there are any stated values at all, they will be proscriptive rather than prescriptive, specifying minimum levels of acceptable conduct rather than aspirational standards to be sought.

The *customer-focused* hierarchy is much more flexible, with people at the lower levels typically empowered to use their initiative in order to advance the customer-is-king ethic. Nordstrom exhorts individuals to use their best judgment; Rank-Xerox allows customer-interface staff to give refunds of up to £200 without reference upwards. Despite apparent convergence of purpose, such organisations can suffer painful tensions internally, as departments compete to interpret the ethical values in a manner favourable to themselves, even if it means that they dissipate some of their energies in fighting the 'enemy' within. The finance function is preoccupied with delivery of share-holder value; the HR function wants a generous budget for staff development. Both may claim ownership of the ethical high ground. To resolve such issues, it makes sense to produce some collectively-generated ethical values and to clarify, in effect, the superordinate goals.

People-focused organisations concentrate on service outside and relationships inside. The corporate vocabulary is peppered with ideas like sharing, caring, co-operation, cohesion, team-work, team-building – almost as if process is more important than outcomes. Within such organisations, the word 'ethics' is often mentioned and ethical values are earnestly examined.

The three categories of organisation – profit-focused,

customer-focused, people-focused – are not mutually exclusive. Indeed, we argue that they should not be, and that a truly powerful company is successful at integrating all three. However, the model does help to explain why some organisations have moved faster than others in showing concern for ethical values and in doing something about it, while others watch from the sidelines or (metaphorically) hurl cynical abuse about the futility of the exercise.

The profit-focused organisation is interested in ethical leadership only to the extent that it may generate increased business, or seems necessary as a defensive marketing exercise. The customer-focused organisation reacts to the ethical priorities of its major customer segments. The people-focused organisation reflects the ethical concerns of its employees. Ethical leadership for the people-focused and customer-focused cultures is likely to be more inspirational and charismatic, particularly if it is to be effective in changing behaviour. Concern for ethical issues, in all three scenarios, may sometimes be conscious in intent and at other times may emerge for what seem to be unlikely reasons. On the whole, the organisations which feel the heat, in ethical terms, are the ones seeking to move from one cultural paradigm to another – finding, to their apparent amazement, that they have unleashed employee-power to a degree which was never anticipated when the process was begun, or that they have mobilised their customers into a cohesive action group.

Producing explicit values, whatever the type of organisation involved, does not necessarily mean that anyone will subscribe to those values. Even the people who wrote them – within the top management team – may lack commitment if their motives are purely instrumental. Perhaps this explains the position of a company known to us which has a mission statement known to its customers but concealed from its employees. If explicit values are generated in circumstances of extreme corporate stress, moreover, there is a greater likelihood that they will be imposed, with corresponding damage to any goals of ownership. Phillips Petroleum illustrates the point, and also shows how the damage can be repaired. In the late 1980s, a planner at Phillips suspected that the management was not particularly committed to the corporate values. His confidential question-naire confirmed these suspicions: many of the company's executives had not participated in drafting the values, did not know where they came from and, as a result, felt little commitment towards them.

The Phillips CEO was initially angry, but then organised a two-day retreat for the top 25 officers of the corporation. One of the most significant products of that meeting was a list of values and beliefs, collectively generated instead of being owned exclusively by the CEO. These values and beliefs included the following propositions:

- treating one another with respect
- giving equal opportunity to every employee
- maintaining a safe working environment
- conducting ourselves ethically and responsibly
- communicating openly and honestly
- supporting individual creativity and innovation
- providing our customers with top quality and services
- protecting the environment
- contributing to the quality of life wherever we operate.

Influences on corporate values

The range of influences on corporate values is immense. For some companies, religion has been the driver – Quaker beliefs for Cadbury and C & J Clark, the Presbyterian Church for Cargill Inc, Mormonism for Novell. For others, the personality of the founder has been crucial in setting the organisational tone (the John Lewis Partnership, Kwik–Fit).

Within some organisations the ethical values are tradition-ally capitalistic, reflecting the single-minded pursuit of wealth without too much regard for any particular moral, ethical, religious or even legal codes. Particularly interesting in this respect has been the behaviour of firms which have knowingly broken the law and paid the penalties, having calculated that the punishments are outweighed by the rewards. With Sunday trading, companies like Tesco and Homebase deliberately infringed the legal constraints, knowing that (a) the sanctions were not crippling, (b) there was always a strong possibility that the sanctions would not be applied anyway, and (c) the experience of shopping on Sundays would create a groundswell of support that would eventually feed its way to the legislators. For Marks & Spencer and the John Lewis Partnership, on the other hand, the same 'facts' were available but were overriden by the kind of social ethic principles that we outlined in Chapter 1.

Sunday trading is an instructive example from other viewpoints, too, because it shows how ethical views in society can change. Three generations ago, any proposals for shops to open on Sundays would have been unthinkable. Today, we complain about the fact that shops of over 3000 square feet have to close on Easter Sunday.

A particularly powerful, if somewhat negative, influence causing organisations to inspect and modify their values is a 'there-but-for-the-grace-of-God' sensation arising from the publicity given to the great ethical disasters like Morton Thiokol's contribution to the Challenger debacle, the Exxon Valdez affair, Bhopal, thalidomide, and Hoover's 'free flights' offer. To illustrate the point we will briefly discuss the actions of Turner & Newall (now known as T&N), once the largest asbestos producer in the UK. Newall's insulation factory at Washington, Tyne and Wear, closed down in 1980. As far back as 1958, however, the factory was regularly provided with evidence of the links between asbestos and mesothelioma (an asbestos-related, incurable cancer of the chest). It had chosen to ignore or suppress the information, so its employees continued to work there oblivious to the dangers. The issue received significant publicity in a BBC2 television documentary shown in April 1994, where it was revealed that at one time T&N had said, in response to claims pursued by the widows and widowers of former T&N workers, that it had retained no historical records concerning the erstwhile labourforce at Washington.

Subsequently it became known that New York lawyers acting on behalf of Chase Manhattan Bank – in litigation with T&N over the cost of stripping asbestos from its 60-floor building – had unearthed more than a million relevant documents from the T&N headquarters in Manchester.

This is just one instance of the damage which can be done when a company makes mistakes, refuses to admit that it has done so and, of course, continues to deny liability. The consequential damage to the firm's reputation is made worse if it appears that there may have been deliberate concealment of information which, had it been available, might have caused employees to act differently.

It would clearly be preferable for organisations to prevent disasters proactively. This is not a Utopian prescription. It would involve a massive shift in ethical values for organisations dominated by fear, given that the vast majority of corporate disasters occur because of negative information blockages. To put it crudely, people with bad news are reluctant to transmit it upwards in case they suffer the fate of the Roman messenger.

Values targeted towards significant stakeholders

We have already outlined our reservations about stakeholder theory (see Chapter 3). Even if we avoid terms like 'stakeholder', however, we have to accept that all organisations reflect a wide variety of interest groups: some of them beneficiaries (in Argenti's terms) and some of them not; some of them supportive and some of them not; some of them enduring and some of them not.

A corporate code of ethical values which addresses one group but ignores others will send out confused messages. Ethical rules aimed solely at employees will make the company appear introspective, and may prompt unhealthy speculation on the unethical actions which prompted such attempts to shut the stable door. Ethical rules concentrating on customers make more sense. This is the principal thrust of Sir Adrian Cadbury's *Harvard Business Review* article in which he argues that the profitable satisfaction of customers should be the overriding moral imperative. If this is done, claims Cadbury, then the creation of jobs cannot be the aim of the organisation as well. Not to place customers first means that they will be denied the benefits of progress, shareholders will be short-changed – and in the long run jobs will be lost anyway.[7]

Our argument, in short, is that a code of ethical values should consist of some comprehensive, wide-ranging principles, followed by equally comprehensive operational guidelines enabling managers and employees to translate these principles into their everyday working lives.

Some organisations spell out their values as pithily as possible, leaving interpretation to individuals. One of the most succinct we have seen is the 'credo' for the US company, Cooper Tires, which reads (in full):

Good merchandise, fair play and a square deal.

Quigley[8] comments that although Cooper has only 2.5 per cent of the replacement tyre market in the USA, it consistently achieves a return on equity approaching 20 per cent, nearly twice the industry average: 'Their approach is simple, uncomplicated, and it works.'

In other instances, so-called ethical value statements read more like instruction books and procedure manuals. TSB Trust's behaviour guidelines embrace such topics as the notification of dangerous situations at work, care for personal possessions, the use of staff identity cards, procedures for welcoming visitors, what to do when a fire is discovered, and access restrictions to certain buildings.

These two extremes show that there are no universal rules for the production of ethical values, apart from the concentration on integrity, honesty, fairness and openness as keynote criteria. Whatever the degree of detail, whatever the priorities, whatever the range of ethical issues addressed, there are nonetheless four key features if ethical value statements are to be more than bland, vacuous 'motherhoods':

- the ideas need to be simple and accessible
- the values should be capable of being shared at all levels
- clear (aspirational) goals for improvement or attainment should be specified
- there must be potential for measuring progress.

Summary

Here we have looked at the contribution of values to the framework for ethical leadership. We cannot stress too emphatically the benefits to be gained from articulating both the values of the ethical leader, and the values to be displayed by the organisation. Bringing the values into the open – rather than treating them as some form of 'background noise' – causes them to be challenged, defended, and reinforced. If ethical values represent the lynchpin of ethical leadership, then once they have been agreed the ethical leader can move forward, translating ideas into action. Implementing ethical leadership is the theme of the next chapter.

References

1. Joseph V. Quigley, *Vision – How Leaders Develop It, Share It, and Sustain It*, New York, McGraw Hill, 1993, p. 21.
2. Ethics Resource Center, *Implementation and Enforcement of Codes of Ethics in Corporations and Associations*, New York, 1980.
3. Cited in Midi Berry and William Keyser, 'Business and ethics' in

Ralph Stacey, (ed.), *Strategic Thinking and the Management of Change*, London, Kogan Page, 1993, p. 154.

4. Robert H. Waterman, Jr, Thomas J. Peters, and Julien R. Phillips, 'Structure is not organisation', *Business Horizons*, June 1980, pp. 24–25.

5. See Gerald Vinton, 'Business ethics: busy body or corporate conscience?' *Leadership and Organisation Development Journal*, Vol. II, No. 3, 1991, pp. 10–11.

6. Cited in Midi Berry and William Keyser, *op. cit.*, p. 156.

7. Sir Adrian Cadbury, 'Ethical managers make their own rules', *Harvard Business Review*, September–October 1987, pp. 67–73.

8. Joseph V. Quigley, *op. cit.*, p. 20.

6

Effective Implementation of Ethical Principles

Introduction

In this chapter we begin to examine the processes to turn ethical values into ethical behaviour. Looking first at some ways of getting it wrong, we then survey key criteria for effective implementation. In particular we stress the need for involvement rather than imposition, mechanisms for the reduction of whistle-blowing, measurement and monitoring, and the crucial significance of the board for role-modelling purposes. Further mechanisms for 'making it happen' through training and HR are discussed in Chapters 7 and 8.

To us, thinking about ethical leadership stems from the realisation that we now live, work, and manage within organisations which are typically more autonomous, more empowered, more delayered, less rule-bound, less individualistic, less static. It is no accident that statements about vision and ethical values have coincided almost everywhere with the collapse of large-scale bureaucracies. True, a vision, some ethical values, and a code of conduct may partially compensate for losing the comfortable, predictable existence associated with conventional hierarchies. On the other hand, an ethical-values framework by itself is nothing more than a skeleton. It needs some flesh, blood, sinews, and intelligence if it is to come alive.

How to get it wrong

Ethical values have to be 'simple enough to be communicated and understood in terms that affect choices of behaviour.'[1] If the ethical values are vague or, worse, appear to be quite different from how staff see their superiors behaving, then the effort will be unproductive. David P. Schmidt's article about a US bank[2] brings the contract between 'hype' and reality into prominent relief.

The bank had created an impressive set of ethical guidelines covering external relationships with customers, communities, and competitors, as well as internal relationships among employees. These ethical values had the benefit of being presented in general terms, unlike the more detailed, compliance-orientated standards of practice common to financial institutions. Also, they were presented as positive, aspirational ideas, not necessarily as descriptions of operational reality:

- We are tireless in or quest to improve quality.
- We treat our customers in a professional manner.
- We strive for honest, candid and prompt communications.
- We prize teamwork, not lone efforts.
- We honour our commitments.

While these principles were officially endorsed by the bank, its managers perceived some discrepancies between them and the actions of some bank executives. The discrepancies could have been explained by the fact that the ethical values were deliberately aspirational. Unfortunately, this was forgotten by those fond of claiming, 'We say we believe in these values, but many times we don't *live* these values, in our actions and in our policies.'

Some years ago, Shell UK's refining operation set out to create an atmosphere of mutual trust and confidence in order to alleviate its industrial relations and staffing problems. The Tavistock Institute was brought in to help create a new philosophy of management, and generous resources were allocated. Later evaluation, however, showed little evidence of the hoped-for changes in behaviour, for the following reasons:

- Most of the recipients didn't understand the message.
- They didn't trust the message anyway because what was being said was so different from the way management had behaved in the past.

- Top-management support waned rapidly as the difficulties of achieving tangible outcomes became apparent.

What we can learn from these examples is that the ethical leader's success depends significantly on resolving problems associated with the management of change. Ethical leaders – no matter how ethical – should avoid these common mistakes:

- insensitivity to the manner in which any change impacts upon the psychological contract of employees
- failure to periodically diagnose the current psychological contract with various groups of employees. As a result, management appears to be out of touch with what these groups expect to offer or receive from the organisation.
- failure adequately to communicate and explain the change to employees. In the absence of any credible and convincing rationale for a sudden concern about ethics, staff may well draw inaccurate and misleading conclusions about why it is being done and what it means for them.

How to get it right

As with any other change, developing and implementing ethical values has to be managed. Publishing some ethical values and an associated code of conduct is the easy part. Naively, some think that publication is enough; they should know better. They must have noticed in the past that making an announcement about some new policy or procedure is no guarantee that anything will happen. Relying on announcements alone generates a virtual certainty that, after a short period of anarchy and speculation, things will carry on as before.

Now this may be fine if the originators of the new ethical values never intended it to be taken seriously. Obvious cynicism among upper management will breed further cynicism (with knobs on) at lower levels. Discrepancies between ethical values and unethical conduct will be noticed by shareholders, customers, and suppliers, who may then elect to take their funds or business elsewhere.

Making the effort to produce some ethical values should justify the extra effort needed to translate aspirations into reality. There are several steps needed: to motivate for change, to manage the transition, and to shape the political dynamics of the change.

Establishing a foundation for change

It has to be shown that pressure for creating ethical values has come from somewhere. The source may be the appointment of a new chief executive with a strong commitment to ethical leadership. Alternatively, management may be able to point to some aspects of the organisation's performance which are contrary to what should be expected. The data may be derived from surveys showing high levels of disgruntlement among significant and powerful stakeholders. Sometimes the stimulus for change is a single piece of adverse publicity, affecting a whole industry or a key player, but prompting offensive ('we are different from the others') and defensive ('we are different from ourselves') action.

Occasionally pressure for ethical values is a by-product of the quality certification search, or it arises from the recognition that the organisation's existing conduct is out of alignment with society's prevailing expectations and with the ethical practices displayed by competitors.

Without a solid foundation for change, nothing will ever begin.

Soliciting employee input and involvement in developing the ethical values

As we saw with the example of Phillips Petroleum cited in Chapter 5, even where the inspiration for ethical values originates with an ethical leader, this does not mean that ethical values can simply be imposed as a *fait accompli*. Some elements of participation in the change will reduce resistance and also build ownership.

Allowing time for adjustment to and internalisation of the new values

Unless ethical values are being generated in a climate of imminent organisational death, then providing time to adjust is not an outrageous luxury. People need to disengage from the existing ways of doing things. The process of disengagement depends on strong communications about

- the importance of the new ethical values and any associated code of conduct
- why the organisation has chosen this moment to make things explicit. Negative as well as positive arguments need to be presented, with no holds barred – especially if 'openness' and 'integrity' are among the behaviours being sought.
- what the ethical values mean for managerial and employee actions.

Managing the transition

A comprehensive vision of the future must be linked closely with the ethical values. If people can't see the logical connections it will be for one of two reasons:

- There aren't any – in which case the whole design process has to be revised.
- They have not been adequately articulated – an issue for the communicators.

Throughout, it is important to stress continuity and the way the ethical values build on what has gone before, rather than representing a radical break with the past.

During implementation, the organisation should appoint an individual with sole responsibility for driving the process forward. Conventionally, this is a role for the HR director, but much depends on whether HR is perceived as a key strategic contributor. In Chapter 4 we briefly discussed some of the issues surrounding single-person responsibility for implementing and sustaining ethical guidelines. Our point then, and repeated now, is that the credibility attached to the whole exercise is greater if high-level ownership is accepted by some senior figure in a more direct 'line' role – especially for organisations where HR has been marginalised.

'Market research' is particularly crucial within the launch and dissemination phases. Managers responsible for embedding the ethical values should develop feedback mechanisms to provide them with data about the effectiveness of the programme – the extent to which it is being taken seriously, whether there are any internal contradictions not previously identified, and the issues generating the most queries about implementation. In SmithKline Beecham's 'Simply Better' campaign, for example, the core value of 'integrity' consumed significantly more managerial and employee attention than the other four values put together.

Involving corporate members in the implementation

It makes sense to seek active, hands-on contributions from every part of the organisation. Key ingredients are

- ensuring support from individuals and groups with significant political power
- using credible and influential figures within the organisation as persuasive communicators. If they are conspicuously on board, employees are more likely to be convinced that the new ethical values are not simply some PR rhetoric.

- incorporating symbols, stories, and specific language within the ethical values to enable them to be woven into the company's operating fabric. Stories and anecdotes help to flesh out what can otherwise appear little more than bland generalisations.
- an incessant communication programme, achieving continuity through existing channels
- creation of simultaneous 'loose–tight' approaches to the creation and adoption of ethical values. Union Carbide has developed one corporate code encompassing ethical conduct, mission and values, but has allowed parts of the organisation to prepare their own statements to address issues of specific local relevance. We should also mention a similar approach used by Stanley Kalms at Dixons.
- the creation of imaginative, resonant catchphrases or brand names for the ethical values and code of conduct packages. 'Five Keys to Self-Renewal' and 'Vision 2000' have already been used, though that doesn't stop them being used again. In our view, 'Simply Better' is preferable to 'Simply the Best', even though the latter does permit management conferences to be accompanied by loud background music from Tina Turner. 'Simply Better' implies a continuous journey and never-ending improvement; 'Simply the Best' suggests complacency and even smugness.
- the CEO must lend vocal support, physical presence and role-modelling to the process. If there is to be a corporate-ethics or business-conduct committee, the CEO should preside over it.
- to keep up the momentum, and to emphasise the organisation-wide significance of the ethical values, it is advisable to create a special cross-functional 'ethical values project team' of mid-level people. The team's broad mandate is to develop strategies for helping the organisation to behave ethically. It is important that this project team is *not* a working party; it must have clear parameters, objectives and milestone paths, and a life expectancy of no more than three to six months.

Defining the rewards for conspicuous compliance and the sanctions for improper conduct

Quite simply, we believe that people do what is rewarded, and avoid doing that which is punished. If ethical values and codes of conduct are promoted without any incentives attached, they will die. In the next chapter we explore possible reward, recognition and punitive systems at greater length.

Establishing effective education and training programmes

Again this issue will be examined in more detail in Chapter 7. The principles behind training programmes geared to acceptance of the ethical values, however, are as follows:

General features: brevity, opportunities for participation, and respect for the experience and intelligence of delegates. Training programmes should not be artificially prolonged, should avoid sermonising, and must not be seen as patronising or naive.

Professional and serious: a 'top-down' sequence is preferable to any 'bottom-up' pattern. The trainers must be credible as trainers as well as being credible by virtue of their organisational positions and reputations. If consultants are used, their material must be totally integrated into the client's culture and, preferably, reinforced by the active presence of in-house professionals.

Mandatory: the universal significance and impact of the ethical values and code of conduct have to be emphasised through comprehensive exposure to training and indoctrination.

Grounded in reality: the content of training programmes must be meaningful to the majority. This will not happen if case-studies and exercises focus largely on the ethical dilemmas confronted by top management when making strategic choices, as opposed to middle management handling day-to-day, largely operational issues.

Publicising achievements and progress

Every effort to blow the trumpet about success must be seized – especially when there is clear evidence that the ethical values have generated some positive benefits for the business.

An 'open' door approach for resolving employee concerns

Some people will need advice, clarification, interpretation or guidance. These issues often derive from personal conflicts over proper business conduct, related to the ethical values. At times, too, employees want to raise concerns about the actions of other employees or the organisation's own policies and actions.

The ethical values cannot provide comprehensive solutions. The best they can do is to establish avenues through which constructive outcomes can be pursued. We firmly believe that providing such avenues is in the best interests of the organisation. If employees are not allowed to ask questions, or are discouraged from doing so, then the repercussions will be serious. Inconsistencies of behaviour emerge: staff become alienated, and their energies are concentrated on covert non-compliance.

If there are no mechanisms for articulating questions, criticisms, or feedback, organisations lose the chance to solve problems and learn from mistakes. Our argument here is virtually identical to that often used about the benefits of soliciting complaints from customers and suppliers. Without feedback, we may never know what we are dong wrong; all we know is that we are losing 'customers' and upsetting our 'suppliers'. If handling complaints and feedback positively is a powerful tool for tying customers and suppliers more closely to us, then finding avenues for two-way communication about the ethical values is an essential ingredient in their adoption and reinforcement.

What is worse, if there are no legitimised outlets for discussion of complex ethical issues, then there are no opportunities for the resolution of improper or unethical corporate conduct. The result is that high-minded employees, learning of such conduct, may expose it publicly through whistle-blowing. Some writers have pointed out that many instances of product liability – from the Ford Pinto fuel-tank to the McDonnell-Douglas DC-10 baggage-door and the 'O' ring on the Challenger Six spacecraft – could have been avoided if the concerns of ethical employees had been listened to whilst the products were still in the development phase.

The ethical values should always advise employees to seek advice in ethically ambiguous situations. Levels of moral reasoning and judgment are likely to be higher when managers get together and discuss ethical issues than when the choices are made in solitude.

One of the advantages of establishing procedures to resolve ethical dilemmas is that the organisation can ensure consistency in the application of the ethical values. It does not matter whether the channel takes the form of the HR department, an internal ombudsman, ethics hotline, a business-conduct committee, the internal audit function, the legal department, or (especially within financial services) a compliance office. In all instances, clear accountability produces powerful benefits in the form of unified messages, even if the price paid is a measure of bureaucratisation.

In practice, whatever formal procedures may dictate, employees faced with ethical issues will often turn to their line managers. Many documents about ethical values recognise this reality, arguing that the manager should act as a filter. Susan Newell[3] is not impressed:

> It is no good suggesting that the employee turns to [his or]
> her supervisor, as it is often this person who is reinforcing
> the unethical behaviour.

Clearly Newell's position has force. For this reason we believe that even if employees are encouraged to raise issues with their immediate seniors, they must also be supplied with alternative mechanisms like an ethics committee which can examine problems more dispassionately.

Some companies have approaches which sound as if they are deliberately trying to deter potential queries, like the bank which advises any employee with an ethical issue to submit a request in writing, with supporting data, to the immediate department manager and the group managing director; following their approval, the request can be submitted to the human resources director and the corporate managing director. By contrast, other companies have less intimidating approaches, making greater use of managers in the front line, especially for problems originating among newer employees.

Requiring managers to give advice on ethical issues persuades them to take the whole thing seriously. They cannot simply refer their staff to some third party and absolve themselves of responsibility. On the other hand, if handling ethical dilemmas is to become a new managerial competence, then it follows that managers must be given the means to enable them to acquire and exercise competency. This means:

- *education* in the ethical values, their rationale, and their action implications
- *training* in process and outcome skills.

If education and training for managers are ignored or under-resourced, managers will not perform effectively. Once again, negative messages will be unintentionally transmitted about the real significance of the ethical values.

Many organisations encourage employees to take advantage of 'open door' access through successively higher levels of management as a means of resolving ethical or business conduct difficulties. The 'open door' procedures themselves vary. At Hewlett Packard, people can go through the hierarchy until they reach the chairman. IBM's 'open door' policy is a flexible response system wholly integrated into the firm's culture: employees may select a supervisor, a manager or an executive to consult, or may leapfrog every level if they would prefer to approach the chairman direct. IBM's goal is to ensure that every ethical question is answered fully, or the dilemma resolved, and the process continues until an acceptable answer is produced.

In the overall context of handling ethical queries, we need to make some points about the principles which should underpin the procedures involved. Thomas[4] cites the Tjosvold classification of three alternatives:

- to 'avoid expressing opposing position or to smooth them over by indicating that they are essentially similar.'[5] If this is the character of management responses to ethical queries, the anxieties and uncertainties associated with debate and argument are avoided in favour of a misleading and artificial sense of agreement. Recipients of the smoothing-over strategy will often recognise that the real issues have been swept under the carpet. Not only have their doubts and questions not been addressed, but they now feel the anger associated with people who know they have been patronised.

- to engage in unproductive confrontation, where the issues are recognised and discussed, but in a closed-mind, dogmatic, threatening, and aggressive fashion. The only purpose of dialogue, according to this stance, is to 'win'.

- an open-minded consideration of relevant viewpoints, coupled with a willingness to incorporate the ideas of others where there seems to be a convincing rationale for doing so. The disputants must be prepared to explore and understand opposing arguments so that, 'after a thorough exploration of opposing positions and their justifications, they are better able to appreciate the shortcomings of their own perspective, integrate useful aspects of other positions into their own, and develop a fresh viewpoint that is responsive to the reasoning and perspectives of others.'[6]

The third approach is more mature and itself reflects the sentiments likely to be inherent within an organisation's ethical values. For it to work then, in turn, three conditions have to be fulfilled:

Goal interdependence: the parties perceive themselves to share a common interest in resolving the ethical issue, rather than being outright opponents locked in mortal combat.

Confirmation: people in the organisation need to feel that when challenging the views of others, or being challenged themselves, their competence is not being called into question. This being so, even difficult ethical questions can be approached with some tolerance and humility.

Collaborative orientation: people in the organisation accept that it is not their role to control the thinking or behaviour of others, but rather to influence by persuasion.

Removing the need for whistle-blowing

We define whistle-blowing as the process of stepping outside one's work role in order to use irregular or external channels of communication to publicise suspected wrongdoing.

The motives of whistle-blowers need not concern us greatly, though investigation of the causes can sometimes be invaluable in suggesting preventive measures. Some hope that recourse to the media will create pressure which will force the organisation to mend its ways. Others wish to express their disapproval of some corporate initiative, or to distance themselves from it – as if the transmission of anonymous letters to a newspaper somehow reduces their 'guilt'. A few whistle-blowers are activated solely by malice, jealousy, resentment, or envy, their aim being to retaliate against others who (as they see it) have made their lives miserable.

Speaking out about matters of conscience is now common-place, especially among professional employees whose loyalty to their profession takes precedence over commitment to the organisation. In our judgment, *every instance of whistle-blowing is evidence of the failure of ethical leadership:*

- the failure to supply channels of communication that would enable dissatisfied employees to articulate their concerns officially
- the failure to take such concerns seriously when they are expressed but, instead, to denigrate the issue, to patronise the employee, to deny the legitimacy of the points being addressed, or to ignore the complaints presumably in the hope that they will subside
- the failure, more broadly, to recognise that organisations can no longer be operated effectively with a command-and-control mentality.

Instead of looking into the issue raised, or seeking to generate more open channels of communication which future whistle-blowers could use, many organisations engage in *ad hominem* abuse of the disaffected employee. Sometimes the alleged wrongdoing will be denied, with denials being produced far more quickly than would have been possible had the issue been investigated. The organisation will introduce 'silence' clauses into employment contracts, yet often without supplying any legitimised opportunities for self-expression. The original whistleblower will seldom be rewarded. None of this behaviour has much to do with ethical leadership, in our view.

Accessible, credible and supportive communication channels are essential if whistle-blowers are to have less justification for resorting to actions producing negative fallout for the organisation. These steps include:

(1) the policy that every employee has the right to express opinions
(2) effective outlet opportunities, including 'open door' policies and speedy responsive processes. These help to diffuse hostility and show concern for resolving ethical dilemmas – especially in organisations like hospitals where so many employees are activated by a 'professional' ethos.
(3) tolerance of dissent.

In *People Management*'s May 1995 article on business ethics[7] Jane Pickard suggested that only two British companies are known to have confidential ethics hotlines for employees to report concerns over ethical issues. The organisations are National Westminster Bank and Lucas Aerospace. Their experience reinforces the views of US companies, where hotlines are well established. Many of the calls simply ask for guidance and people can receive immediate answers or be referred elsewhere. Just occasionally, major pieces of misconduct are mentioned, justifying the claim that the hotline works to produce less external whistle-blowing.

In NatWest, many of the questions are apparently about gifts and hospitality, whether there are any cash limits and what it is sensible to accept. Most hotline issues are resolved locally, although the trends are reported to the board. NatWest monitors the effectiveness of its ethics programme more broadly, too, by looking at staff disciplinary cases and staff/supplier attitude-survey results. Ethical information is available over the Bank's corporate information computer network, and the monitoring of ethical performance is one of the non-financial measures on which the NatWest Group evaluates itself.

Monitoring and measuring adherence to ethical values

In searching for uniformity in the application of ethical values, some companies have created committees or ombudsmen whom employees can call upon to resolve questions or report improper practices. Unisys favours the ombudsman approach, using a senior executive from the legal department who advises the company on ethics matters and administers the corporate hotline through which employees can anonymously seek guidance and advice. The hotline can also be used for reporting any possible violations of the law or of the company's ethics.

A specifically-constituted ethics or business conduct committee is helpful as a final authority for responding to questions about ethics, and for ensuring compliance. Establishing such a committee offers several advantages:

- It sends out signals about the importance of the ethical values.
- The committee may adjudicate on issues which are too controversial for top management comfortably to decide alone.
- It provides the chairman or CEO with a separate forum for discussion of ethical or business-conduct issues.
- It can furnish moral support for those who seek advice or want to report ethical concerns.
- It supplies a fresh perspective, objectivity and fairness, especially if some of its members are outsiders (like non-executive directors, retained consultants, or specially-recruited independent representatives). If it reports to the board, too, the committee has some protection against undue managerial influence.

A special case is the procedure used in the John Lewis Partnership. Thirty-two 'registrars' provide confidential advice to employees as well as a two-way information bridge between managers and employees. The 'registrars', accountable directly to the chairman, and securely independent of other managers, operate hotlines in between visits to various John Lewis branches, and will even meet employees on neutral territory away from their workplaces, if necessary. The John Lewis house magazine, too, has a well-established policy of publishing virtually all employee correspondence and for requiring satisfactory responses from senior managers. With such outlets available, it may be no accident that whistle-blowing is unknown in the John Lewis Partnership.

Many organisations seek to reinforce and reinvigorate their ethical values by requiring employees to sign annual certificates. Sometimes, too, compliance forms are certified annually and specify that employees should disclose any ethical values and conduct-code violations which they have witnessed, or of which they have knowledge, or to which they have been a party.

Certification of this kind can easily give the impression that the organisation has become a police state. A focus on mere compliance is negative, too, and scarcely reflects the obligations of ethical leadership. It may mean that employees devote considerable time and energy to producing behaviour which complies only minimally with the published criteria, especially if they believe the compliance criteria have been externally imposed and enjoy little more than lip-service endorsement within the company. Compliance rules are often seen not as positive assets but rather as unjustified restrictions preventing or inhibiting the proper exercise of entrepreneurial initiative. Under such circumstances there is unlikely to be an atmosphere of continuous improvement surrounding the ethical values and the code of conduct. Nor is it probable that all the systems, structures and procedures within the organisation will be proactively aligned to support right behaviour choices or penalise inappropriate ones. There may even be a degree of managerial connivance about deviations from the ethical values, if it is believed that the chances of discovery are non-existent.

On the other hand, certification is a powerful deterrent to indefensible actions. Where people have to sign a statement every year to confirm that they have not violated the ethical values, they are likely to take them more seriously. This is particularly so if it is made apparent that the signatures have contractual implications.

Measuring the effectiveness of ethical values

Besides written assurances of commitment by employees, the ethical leader uses surveys, questionnaires, and periodic audits to measure compliance with ethical prescriptions. Companies adopting such methods include Peugeot Talbot, Yorkshire Bank, Costain, Dixons, Rolls-Royce, and IBM.

The audit approach is preferred by organisations like Abbey National and BT. Trained auditors bring impartiality, independence, and considerable knowledge of the organisation's business to the process of evaluating compliance and suggesting opportunities for continuous improvement – especially if they are already familiar with benchmark or 'best practice' innovations pioneered elsewhere.

Some companies rely on internal auditors and line managers acting in an auditor role. In Hewlett Packard, the audit group annually interviews the top managers from each of the firm's corporate groups. The auditors pose a battery of questions seeking to establish familiarity with HP's values, its code of conduct, the frequency and depth of communication the manager has had with other employees regarding the code, and degrees of awareness about any ethical violations or government sanctions against the part of the organisation for which each manager is responsible.

By themselves, ethical values do not represent measurable commodities. Neither do the Ten Commandments. If adherence (or otherwise) to the Ten Commandments can be measured through various derived indices, then so too can ethical values. In effect, ethical values are the 'theory' through which 'empirical hypotheses' can be developed – usually by deductive thought processes; support for the 'empirical hypotheses' can then be construed as endorsement of the 'theory', the over-arching conceptual framework.

Nor is it impossibly difficult to translate ethical values into key performance areas and measurable objectives for significant director, executive and managerial players in the organisation. We shall look at the possibilities at greater length in Chapter 9.

The role of the board, and role-modelling by board members

The short answer to the question 'Who is responsible for making sure that the organisation's ethical values come alive? is 'Everyone who works for the organisation.' Yet this response is too glib, too facile, totally unconvincing. If everyone in the organisation had equal power and influence, it might just have some credibility. In practice, some people have more power than others.

The board as a group is of special significance. The person scrutinised most of all, with every word dissected, analysed and subjected to detailed semantic investigation, will be the chief executive (plus the chairman, if there is one).

According to Colin Coulson-Thomas, 'It is difficult for a "sense of what is right" to thrive elsewhere and pervade a company, if it is absent from the boardroom.'[8]

The chairman is the person best equipped to form an overview of the board and its operations. He is therefore responsible for ensuring that the board plays its part in formulating, agreeing, sharing and implementing the values. Two pertinent questions for the chairman are

- Are your directors committed to the values and their implementation? Which of them are paying lip-service or are just along for the ride?
- How effective are the board members at sharing the values, communicating them downwards and with customers?

One chief executive refers to 'fellow-traveller' directors, saying, 'I lived for too long with directors who did not really believe in what we were trying to do. They didn't raise objections in the boardroom. What's worse, they sometimes said yes, and then went away and did nothing. They didn't implement the changes in their divisions, and everyone knew it.'[9]

All surveys acknowledge the importance of strong and explicit leadership from the chief executive and the chairman. Other directors and many senior managers are likely to base their own level of commitment on the priority given to the ethical values by these role models – who are role models, incidentally, whether they like it or not, whether they admit it or not, and whether they deny it or not. What is more, the chief executive – perhaps even more than the chairman – can play a key part in preventing the occurrence of 'perspective gaps' and 'arenas of confrontation'.

It needs to be stressed that ethical leadership by itself is not enough. The chief executive's ethical leadership has to be visible and consistent – visible so that nobody can be in any doubt about the CEO's position, and consistent so that nobody can use ambiguity as a pretext for inaction.

References to the position of chairman and CEO lead inevitably to issues surrounding corporate governance and its place in the development, dissemination, and maintenance of the organisation's ethical values.

Just over a decade ago, the phrase 'corporate governance' did not exist. Now it is commonplace. Part of its popularity stems from recognition of some major new dilemmas facing company directors. On the negative side, concern has been stimulated by adverse publicity about corporate gluttony, naked self-interest and greed, especially linked to board-level rewards and the size of pay-offs to departing board members.

Clearly the ethical practices within a corporate board will have an impact on the organisation's ethical values, the mechanisms by which the ethical values are communicated, and the perceived credibility of ethical imperatives among employees and external stakeholders. Hence, consideration of the board's function is relevant to ethical leadership.

In Hilmer's view[10] boards have two distinct roles: *monitoring* (concern for performance) and *performance enhancement*. As monitor, the board's primary task is to ensure that management runs the organisation in the interests of the shareholders and other stakeholders, and in accordance with law. As the stimulus for performance enhancement, the board acts as a driver for change and for continuous improvement: doing new things, doing existing things in new ways, and delivering added value through the constant search for competitive advantage. In the 1970s, concern for monitoring seemed to diminish and writers emphasised performance enhancement; in the 1990s the pendulum has swung back towards monitoring as the key role, largely because of disenchantment with corporate conduct in several countries.

If we look closely at the board's two roles of 'performance enhancement' and 'monitoring', plus the degree to which the roles are carried out conscientiously, then we can generate the typology presented in Figure 6.1 below.

Figure 6.1

Types of boards

Effective monitoring

		No	**Yes**
Effective Performance Enhancement	**No**	*Type 1* • Weak • Split	*Type 2* • Bureaucratic process driven
	Yes	*Type 3* • Network	*Type 4* • Strategic activist • Keiretsu?

Source: Frederick G. Hilmer, 'The governance research agenda: a practitioner's perspective', *Corporate Governance – An International Review*, Vol. 1, No. 1, 1993.

Type 1 reflects the kind of board which is ineffective at both 'monitoring' and 'performance enhancement'. An example is the board dominated by a strong CEO who neither takes counsel nor accepts criticism from subordinates or other directors. The board is composed of sycophants. Board meetings consist of CEO monologues, and quick formal approvals of decisions and results. In terms of ethical leadership, this board supplies none. Its hidden agenda is concerned with the self-preservation and self-aggrandisement of the CEO. The system attracts little criticism so long as the organisation is successful, but it cannot cope with failure, which is always blamed by the CEO on some maliciously-inspired external factors.

If such organisations have a vision and any ethical values, their production is an exercise in pure PR cynicism. In Chapter 3, we reproduced the mission statement for Maxwell Communications plc, headed by Robert Maxwell:

'We aim, by excellence of management and pre-eminence in technology, to grasp the great opportunities created by the ever-increasing worldwide demand for information, prosperity and peace.'

As Foster[11] points out, it did *not* say

'We aim, through the consistent and creative application of double-dealing, contempt, bullying, lying, subterfuge, connivance, theft and fraud, to cheat our investors, our employees, our pensioners, our suppliers and other business partners where we choose to operate, or *die* in the attempt!'

A *Type 2* board is effective at 'monitoring' but ineffective about 'performance enhancement'. Operating typically as checker and policeman, this is a board that knows little about the business, but does know a lot about maintaining tight control. The directors tend to be remote, operating through bureaucratic processes and rituals, carefully observing all external and internally-imposed rules. Such boards may be dominated by outsiders, often accountants or lawyers without significant understanding of the factors underpinning performance, but with high standards of propriety and professional integrity.

Examples of such boards occur in highly-regulated industries (financial services) or in utilities where performance flows from the granting of a licence and the board sees its principal function as ensuring that the licence is not in danger of being revoked. Other instances include long-established firms that continue to live off past successes, or companies with a high market share and other quasi-monopolistic positions which enable them to remain largely immune to competitive pressures.

A 'monitoring' focus will produce ethical values and linked conduct codes which emphasise penalties for deviation – penalties, moreover, which will often be exemplary rather than fitted to the crime. Procedures will be bureaucratic and operations process-driven: it becomes more important to ascertain that everything has been done correctly (ie in accordance with strict guidelines) than to measure whether the outcomes have been beneficial.

Type 3 organisations are effective at 'performance enhancement' but ineffective at 'monitoring'. The CEO chooses people of high ability as directors, but also ensures that they share the CEO's view of the world. Such directors tend to support the managerial authority of the CEO, but can improve decision-making quality because of their differing perspectives and insights. The 'club' atmosphere at board meetings is a positive asset. Members are uninhibited about raising issues or ideas, and conversely the CEO does not feel threatened by raising matters with the board.

In terms of corporate ethics, the 'network board' will be better at producing high-flown rhetoric about ethical values and vision, but will be much less consistent about implementation. Indeed, they may well believe that creating the ideals is

sufficient in itself and that the process of acceptance, internal-
isation, and commitment will follow automatically.

In the fourth box is the 'strategic activist' board, effective at
both 'performance enhancement' and 'monitoring'. This is the
board which supplies a vision but which also seeks to make it
happen.

The strategic activist board is very concerned about ethical
values, since they touch on almost every aspect of the processes concerned with corporate governance. The very phrase,
'strategic activist', implies that there is *not* a stark separation
between (a) the role of the board in creating the ethical values,
and (b) the role of management in delivering them. As gaps
emerge between aspiration and achievement, the strategic
activist board recognises that effort needs to be allocated to
motivating, empowering, and equipping the people of the
organisation to 'make it happen'.

Many organisations and their boards are still far from any
realisation that they need to shift from a command-and-control
culture towards empowerment, sharing, enabling, building
trust and commitment, and the shaping of ethical values within
the organisation to create the kind of corporate renewal
advocated by Robert Waterman[12]. Colin Coulson-Thomas has
identified some of the discriminators between effective and
ineffective boards: these are summarised in Table 6.1. Their
message is salutary and significant for the future of ethical
leadership.

Summary

Our approach to implementing ethical values deliberately
requires further thinking, for we have not spelt out the mechanisms in comprehensive detail. To do so would be misleading
and simplistic. Slavishly copying what some other organisation
has done is dangerous; it is preferable to understand what is
required – mechanisms to offset whistle-blowing, systems for

Table 6.1

The Boardroom Agenda: Positive and Negative Symptoms

Positive symptoms	Negative symptoms
Breakout/transformation	Spiral of descent to marginal commodity supplier status
Long-term focus	Short-term orientation
Redeploy to activities that add value for customers	Headcount reduction
Concern with customer satisfaction	Concern with financial numbers
Investment approach to quality, training, and IT	Preoccupation with costs of training, IT, etc
Build added-value opportunities	Lower price/price competitively
Securing commitment	Wordsmithing
Speed up service to customers to increase customer satisfaction and generate cash	'Screw customers' to increase margins and generate cash
Emphasis on building relationships	Bargaining and negotiation orientation
Empowering and sharing culture	Control culture
Focus on fact, reality and intention	Expressions of opinion, surmise and hope
Holistic approach	'Line-by-line' approach

Source: Colin Coulson-Thomas, *Transforming the Company – Bridging the Gap Between Management Myth and Corporate Reality*, London, Kogan Page, 1992, p. 40.

auditing progress, active involvement of the board – and then generate processes directly customised for the specific company, taking account of size, traditions, competitive position, the balance of stakeholder power, and so forth. Our experience gives us some guidelines for getting it wrong and for getting it right, but within those boundaries there is considerable flexibility for alternative solutions.

Clarifying the issues concerned with whistle-blowing, measurement, and top-management role-modelling were all major themes for Chapter 6. Our next major concerns involve training and the onward cascade of ethical leadership throughout the organisation.

References

1. Charles Baden-Fuller and John M. Stopford, *Rejuvenating the Mature Business – The competitive challenge*, London, Routledge, 1992, p. 168.
2. David P. Schmidt, 'Integrating ethics into organisational networks', *Journal of Management Development*, Vol. 11, No. 4, 1992, pp. 34–43.
3. Susan Newell, *The Healthy Organisation – Fairness, ethics and effective management*, London, Routledge, 1995, pp. 186–187.
4. Alan Berkeley Thomas, *Controversies in Management*, London, Routledge, 1993, pp. 25–27.
5. D. Tjosvold, 'Implications of controversy research for management', *Journal of Management*, Vol. 11, 1985, pp. 21–37.
6. Alan Berkeley Thomas, *op. cit.*, pp. 25–26.
7. Jane Pickard, 'Prepare to make a moral judgment', *People Management*, 4 May 1995, pp. 22–25.
8. Colin Coulson-Thomas, *Creating Excellence in the Boardroom*. Maidenhead, McGraw Hill, 1993, p. 124.
9. Colin Coulson-Thomas, *Transforming the Company – Bridging the gap between management myth and corporate reality*, London, Kogan Page, 1992, p. 45.
10. Frederick G. Hilmer, 'The governance research agenda: a practitioner's perspective', *Corporate Governance – An International Review*, Vol. 1, No. 1, 1993, pp. 26–32.
11. Timothy R.V. Foster, *101 Great Mission Statements – How the world's leading companies run their businesses*, London, Kogan Page, 1993, p. 16.
12. Robert H. Waterman, Jr., *The Renewal Factor*, New York, Bantam, 1987.

7

▩ Supporting Ethics through Training

Introduction

Implementation of ethical values and a code of conduct presupposes a congruence between the standards enshrined within the values and the actual behaviour of the organisation's employees. Ethical values and codes of conduct require an intrinsic accountability, ie individuals must be reasonably comfortable that their actions conform with the expectations outlined by the organisation. This can only be assured when employees are *educated* about the ethical values, their action implications, and the reward/reinforcement/sanction mechanisms intended to prod, push and pull people in the desired direction.

Codes and values which are neither explained to employees, nor enforced, suggest a mere window-dressing document. In fact, education and training about the ethical values are part of a system designed to heighten consciousness about proper conduct for all employees. As an instance of what can be achieved, the ICL statement of beliefs, 'Ten Obligations of the ICL Manager', has been so intensively promoted through training programmes that it has genuinely become a way of life.

Without the kind of common understanding achieved through training, compliance with the ethical values is impossible. The mere presence of a finished set of ethical principles is far from being sufficient to ensure integrity and morality within the organisation. After all, it is individuals who determine, by their conduct, whether the standards reflected in the ethical values will be met or compromised. Showing managers and employees how to behave when faced with conduct or ethical issues, and clarifying the language within the ethical values themselves, has to be a critical need.

135

Ethical reasoning and moral maturity

Although we covered some of these issues in Chapter 4, we now need to look more clearly at the place of ethical values and a code of conduct in the scheme of things. Their purpose is to sensitise people to ethical issues and spell out, in broad terms, the ethical priorities (especially for managers) in the organisation. Less attractive in principle is Benson's claim[1] that many managers are not very good at disciplined ethical reasoning and so need some sort of code to guide them. This may be acceptable in the short term, but surely it would be preferable – indeed, MacLagan[2] sees it as necessary – to train and educate managers so that they are capable of reasoning about moral issues. If this could be accomplished, then some of the purposes for a code of conduct would have been fulfilled, and the code itself would eventually become obsolescent.

The trouble is that many codes of conduct offer employees considerable latitude to choose how they behave, even within the constraints of the ethical principles around which such codes are constructed. If the code states that the organisation will be a good member of the community, people may still be confused about what is meant by the 'community', which parts of it should have precedence, and about ways of dealing with conflicts of interest among various 'community' members and groups. Equally, if ethical values and codes stress the significance of shareholders and employees, which of them should justify preferential treatment when differing priorities present themselves? We have seen this problem before: the ambiguity of language in corporate directives, the internal contradictions in sets of administrative principles, and even the paradoxes presented among proverbs ('Look before you leap' as opposed to 'He who hesitates is lost').

In Chapter 4 we pointed out that a code of conduct may provide employees with an institutional defence against taking personal risks in decision situations. The creation of a code implies that managers and professionals (in particular) cannot be trusted to take morally adequate decisions. This brings us to a point which is more contentious but which has particular significance for the purposes, structure and design of any training processes linked to ethical leadership.

According to Kohlberg,[3] conformity with a code of conduct or with a prescribed set of ethical values represents a lower level of personal moral development than the more independent reasoning which is seen as the alternative. In Kohlberg's view, 'moral maturity' entails three separate competencies:

- a commitment to ideals
- a capacity for moral reasoning
- a capacity to act accordingly.

Kohlberg's model, originally associated with childhood and adolescent development, has subsequently been extended into the world of organisations.[4] The essence of his position is that people can progress through three basic levels of moral development, measured in terms of their capacity to engage in moral reasoning and their willingness to move from purely selfish behaviour to a concern about the treatment of others.

The way in which individuals progress through these three levels has parallels with the post-bureaucratic preference for encouraging employees to be independent-minded, questioning and critical about organisational processes – as a necessary prelude, for instance, to added-value quality enhancement. Pulling in the other direction are the more traditional values of deference to authority and conformity with organisational norms. Companies want their people to be both conforming (in the sense of being loyal and committed to the organisation's survival and growth) yet non-conforming (in the sense that they are prepared to challenge established ways of doing things).

In broad terms, Kohlberg's three levels of moral development are

The preconventional level: individuals adopt reward-seeking, punishment-avoiding behaviour. Except insofar as they can escape detection or sanction, they will follow the rules laid down for them. Reciprocity with others will be confined calculatively to situations where it is seen as instrumental for self-interest purposes.

Conventional role-conformity: loyalty to the prevailing social order is displayed, perhaps simply out of a desire to be one of the crowd, or in order to support the *status quo.*

Principled or autonomous reasoning: this may have a social contract and utilitarian emphasis, in which laws and rules are obeyed on the grounds that they convey 'the greatest good for the greatest number'; or the individual may generate ethical principles reflecting human rights and respect for the dignity of individuals. In Chapter 3, reporting research by Archie Carroll,[5] we noted a considerable variety of ethical options available to managers, professionals and employees, ranging from the 'Golden Rule' to short-run hedonism. Surprisingly to us, Carroll's study suggested that utilitarianism was the least popular of the 11 ethical frameworks supplied.

Carroll shows that 'principled morality' found at this third level need not necessarily indicate that the individual will act in accordance with the organisation's ethical values. 'Consequently,' notes MacLagan,[6] 'such personal principles will be upheld even when in conflict with the concrete norms of the group or organisation.'

When putting together a training package, it is important to recognise the difference between purely cognitive development and emotional commitment to any given set of ethical values. People may intellectually understand, say, the theories behind equal opportunity; it is quite another thing for them to demonstrate conviction or even passion in pursuit of such ends.

Other issues particularly relevant to training specialists concern the blockages which prevent employees from living up to their ideals. Such blockages can result from conflict between personal conscience and the organisation's ethical values, or struggles between differing dimensions of the employee's ethical framework and priorities.

To resolve such dilemmas, people will often rationalise their way out of feeling responsible for the consequences of the actions they take when performing their corporate roles. An obvious example is the conflict between obligations to dependants (implying the need to retain one's job) and the knowledge that one is involved in an organisational activity that is inconsistent with some personal principle.

Dissonance-reducing rationalisation is encouraged by the formal definition of responsibilities, by reference to performance objectives and other 'imperatives' which, conveniently, seem to override the more generalised principles enshrined in any ethical values or a corporate code of conduct. In Chapter 2 we have already discussed Gellerman's framework[7] of four commonly used 'justifications' for unethical behaviour, namely a belief that

- the activity is not really illegal or immoral at all
- the activity is actually in the best interests of the individual and/or the organisation
- the activity is 'safe' because it will never be found out or publicised
- because the action helps the organisation, this will ensure that it is condoned.

Implications for the design of training programmes

No organisation will openly admit that it wants its employees to be emotionally retarded, intellectually unquestioning, behaviourally constrained automatons! On the contrary, the logic of our current concerns for process re-engineering, empowerment, decentralisation, autonomy at the customer interface, and so forth, is linked to these changes[8] occurring in the world of work:

- *work units* – from functional departments to process teams

- *jobs* – from simple tasks to multi-dimensional work
- *roles* – from 'controlled' to 'empowered'
- *job preparation* – from 'training' to 'education'
- *performance* – from activity to results
- *promotion criteria* – from performance to ability
- *values* – from protective to productive
- *managers* – from supervisors to coaches
- *structures* – from hierarchical to flat
- *executives* – from scorekeepers to leaders.

So the ethical leader wants people to think for themselves. This is essential anyway, because it will exemplify the ethical values and also because it will equip employees with the ability to confront ethically the varied situations which arise in the course of their work, but which cannot be covered comprehensively within a code of conduct. Traditional lecture-based approaches will be relevant in making a contribution to the cognitive development processes leading to Kohlberg's level-three competence of 'autonomous reasoning'. However, experiential learning is essential to the achievement of objectives concerned with commitment to ethical values and a code of conduct, together with the ability to apply these frameworks to specific situational scenarios.

Although ethical leadership and organisational practice both imply the capacity to think, the purposes of corporately-inspired training in ethical value and conduct code implementation have to be different from any education about ethics which may take place in business schools. In fact much of the literature about the 'teaching' of ethics is written with a business-school context in mind – especially after the $20m pledge by former Securities and Exchange Commission Chairman John Shad to Harvard Business School to advance the cause of ethics.[9]

When business schools speak of 'sensitising' students to ethical considerations, this is best understood, not as a process of trying to make business-school students ethical, but in the sense of trying to make them aware of what some other people, or organisations, or society at large, take to be important factors in the conduct of business. As a consequence of 'ethics programmes' at business schools, some individuals will learn that behaving ethically can produce business advantage: they will 'adopt' ethical principles for instrumental reasons. Other students may come to accept the desirability of acting ethically 'from the inside', or through Kohlberg's 'autonomous reasoning', rather than simply to satisfy others or to advance themselves.

As Professor Jack Mahoney concedes,[10] 'those who are convinced of the personal need to be ethical in their business dealings will approach the subject with more commitment and therefore more interest. They *may* [author's emphasis] well also do better at it, at least insofar as they have a sympathy for it and might thus have a greater capacity for understanding and insight.'

By contrast with business schools, organisations seeking to secure compliance with and commitment to their ethical values have more specific, action-driven purposes whose outcomes can be more directly measured. To understand some of the techniques and methods which can be used, we look in depth at the experience of one organisation, the Cummins Engine Company.[11]

Ethics training in action at Cummins

Cummins already has a reputation for socially responsible and ethical management, though it concedes that it is not perfect, and problems of sustaining and implementing ethical management arise regularly. Its formal training on ethics and management seeks to provide

- a framework for understanding what 'ethics' is about
- some tools to resolve ethical issues arising at work.

At the same time, the training is not heavily prescriptive and proscriptive. As one would expect from an exercise which is intended to promote 'autonomous reasoning', it is much more than a simple set of do's and don'ts.

The specific goals for the two-day workshop are

- to increase awareness of the ethical dilemmas that surface in everyday corporate life
- to reflect on and sharpen the process which people use to make ethical choices, and to increase understanding about that process
- to understand the frameworks for ethical management at Cummins.

Our view is that these goals could usefully be tightened to address some other issues:

- recognition of the fact that many business decisions, especially at managerial level, involve ethical considerations – in fact the range of such decisions is much larger than participants initially imagine
- realisation that decisions made by corporate employees will contribute to the organisation's ethical environment internally and its reputation externally – and that these factors have a powerful impact on business success.

Within the Cummins programme, lecturing is kept to a minimum and learning is structured around the analysis of cases and group discussion. The case-studies are derived from incidents which have occurred within the company or incidents which are hypothetical but which closely resemble typical Cummins scenarios. The selection of such case-studies is crucial. Participants need to see the situations as being relevant to their experiences and needs. The importance of this point is echoed by Milton Snoeyenbos:[12]

It seems clear that if we want to focus on the ethics

problems that students are likely to encounter, we should
study those problems that actually occur in business from
the perspective of those low in the organisational hierarchy. This is where all employees begin their careers, and
most of them will not rise above middle-management
levels. Yet the cases typically discussed in business ethics
texts . . . address problems faced primarily by top-level
management; Ford's decision to produce the Pinto is often
discussed, as is Lockheed's sale of the Tristar in Japan, a
sale handled primarily by A. Carl Kotchian, Lockheed's
President. While interesting, these are not the sorts of
ethical dilemma which the vast majority of employees will
ever face.

Concentrating on high-level ethical dilemmas, too, may
reinforce the false belief that ethics involves only the extra-
ordinary events of corporate life and not the mundane day-to-
day management of a department, function, or work group.

At Cummins, each workshop is divided into three phases
outlined below.

The first phase, focusing on *what this is about*, includes some
definitions and some background information, so that the
workshop members do not get bogged down in semantics or
frightened off by unfamiliar jargon. Quite frequently, at this
point in any training adventure addressing ethical issues, some
will complain about being indoctrinated or 'preached at', and
others will raise the challenge that 'ethics can't be taught'. On
the first issue, Cummins will readily admit – as most other
organisations would – that a crucial part of the workshop's
purpose is to encourage everyone in the company to subscribe
to, and behave in accordance with, the ethical values and the
code of conduct. There is no point in denying this aim: to do so
would not only infringe the ethical values themselves, but
would also imply some guilt about them. Persuading people
about the benefits of committing themselves to the ethical
values is a perfectly legitimate exercise, where the argument is
founded on the business advantages (for long-term profitability) and the personal benefits (for feelings of self-esteem
and the removal of moral doubt).

Giving employees information can always be construed as 'indoctrination', but this accusation only holds up if

- the information has been deliberately designed to be misleading
- no alternatives are sensibly offered, together with an impartial assessment of their consequences for the organisation and for the individual.

One of the most powerful arguments for behaving ethically, in fact, concerns the probable impact of behaving otherwise. As John Akers has argued,[13] no society can compete very long or successfully with people stealing from one another or not trusting one another, with every bit of information requiring notarised confirmation, with every disagreement ending up in litigation, or with government having to regulate all businesses in order to keep them honest. Unethical behaviour, says Akers, is a recipe for headaches, inefficiency, and waste. History has proved that the greater the trust and confidence of people in the ethics of an institution or society, the greater its economic strength.

So far as the assertion that 'ethics can't be taught' is concerned, one response is to separate out the character and the rational components of ethical behaviour. It is unlikely that a two-day workshop will significantly influence a person's character; but what can be taught are the 'rational' competencies of

- recognising ethical issues
- analysing them from an ethical standpoint
- identifying the choices and their consequences
- selecting one or more from the options available in order to maximise outcomes.

Another angle is to assert that even if ethics cannot be taught, it can certainly be *learned* (just as life assurance is *bought* rather than *sold*). Individuals initially 'learn' about ethical behaviour in the family, and then, as Andrews claims,[14] 'most education in business ethics will occur in the organisations in which people spend their lives.' The trouble with such 'education' is that it is erratic, spasmodic, hit-and-miss, capable of generating false beliefs about what is perceived to be 'right' and 'wrong' in the organisation, and riddled with ambiguities. At least an ethics workshop seeks to produce an integrated framework throughout the organisation.

Phase two at Cummins involves these very frameworks, since it focuses on *models for ordering and analysing ethical situations*. For many companies like Cummins, this will be the heart of the training process, since a key part for phase two will be an outline of the ethical values, the code of conduct, and the organisation's expectations concerning ethical conduct. Crucial to the effectiveness of the training will be

- a willingness to respond openly to all questions, doubts, anxieties, and even scepticism
- explanations about the rationale for developing ethical values and a code
- the supply of specific examples reflecting how the code and values will work in practice.

It is important to reassure employees that the appearance of formal statements about corporate ethics is not necessarily linked to any particular event within the company. On the other hand, if there *are* links between a recent ethical disaster in the organisation and the emergence of a system designed to pre-empt such possibilities in the future, this should not be concealed. Shutting the stable door will not help if the horse has bolted, but there are always other horses which could escape if nothing is done. Our point is that presenting ethical values and a code of conduct as if they are purely reactive is no way to gain acceptance or commitment. The exercise will be viewed as negative window-dressing and even scapegoating, rather than as a positive opportunity to learn from the mistakes of the past in order to improve performance in the future.

Workshops in ethics must also work hard to reassure

participants that they are not being implicitly accused of unethical behaviour. Employees who are members of professional bodies, and who already see themselves as subscribing to systems of professional ethics, can be very defensive on issues of this kind. The line to take – because it is true, not because it is expedient – is that adherence to some explicit ethical values and a code of conduct is beneficial to the people in the organisation, advantageous for its external stakeholders, and ultimately good for the survival of the organisation as a whole: that is why we are doing it. We are doing it, too, because the organisation needs to present a unified ethical face to the world.

The third phase for each Cummins workshop involves *the analysis of cases and situations brought in by the participants*. As the 'price of admission' to the workshop each delegate must submit, in writing, an ethical situation that he or she has encountered or observed. These cases are analysed in syndicates, with recommendations presented in plenary session as a practical application of the tools presented with phase two.

Ethics training of the kind developed at Cummins Engines is only a single component of encouraging behaviour aligned to ethical values. Like all training, its long-term effectiveness depends on a supportive institutional context. To summarise, the essential ingredients include:

Top and senior management commitment – preferably through some physical presence and involvement within the workshops.

Staff support within HR and other service functions – to show concern about ethical conduct and how people are treated.

Constant reiteration of the ethical values – with explanations to show their relevance, application and benefits.

A code of conduct – that supplies a more detailed framework for behaviour (both prescribed and proscribed).

Reinforcement of the values and code through other mechanisms – like induction training and performance review.

Reward and recognition systems – which promote conspicuous and exemplary behaviour.

Other considerations in ethics training

Competent and credible delivery of ethics training, apart from the design of the training itself, is a major issue if organisations are serious about embedding the ethical values and the conduct code into the corporate culture. For the business schools, the picture is confused. Business ethics is not yet a career subject, so leaders of business ethics modules have come from a variety of primary disciplines like marketing, accountancy, economics, organisational behaviour, or law; in a few instances the teaching is brought in from philosophy or theology. Following the Shad pledge, Harvard has recruited a core of four academic staff, originally specialists in other fields but now committed to advancing education and research into business ethics; but Harvard also seeks to integrate ethics into conventional business disciplines. About 40 per cent of Harvard's case-studies on ethics, for example, have been written by professors in such fields as accounting and marketing.

The position for organisations commissioning in-house training (as opposed to ethics education) is naturally quite different. Broadly speaking, there are three options:

- professional in-company trainers
- line managers
- external trainers/consultants.

Each group has its own merits and disadvantages. In-company trainers are likely to be competent communicators and will sing from the same hymn-sheet, as it were. On the other hand, they often lack the degree of credibility required, particularly if they are seen as nothing more than mouthpieces for ideas which have originated elsewhere but whose creators (some will say) are unwilling to project these ideas themselves. Within the organisation there may be powerful groups which will want to put the worst possible construction on this.

The 'trickle-down' approach, using line managers to train their own teams on a cascade basis – perhaps as an extension of the team brief or team meeting concept – has much to commend it. Pioneered by Motorola, the system uses 'trainers' in the first instance (ie, at senior levels) who have strong commitment to the success of the ethical values (particularly if their own performance objectives include compliance criteria). Further, it is normal for managers to enjoy high credibility with their staff. As an example, National Provident Institution's approach involved managers meeting with groups of eight to ten staff; such direct, highly individual contact is equally the norm at Tesco.

Using managers as trainers creates a powerful pressure on the managers to become thoroughly familiar with the ethical values and the conduct code themselves. The training helps to reinforce these ideals with the participating managers, too. The downside is that some managers make better trainers than others – a few, in particular, are not happy about handling questions and objections from their own teams. Of course, this is no reason for allowing these managers to opt out: they must be given training and resources to build up their expertise and competence. What is more, managers have to be coached rigorously towards a positive perspective, in case some feel inclined to display their own initial scepticism by such throw-away remarks as 'As you know, the Company in its infinite wisdom has decreed that from today we are supposed to work within a framework of these ethical values . . .'

The main advantage of using outside trainers or consultants is the assurance that the training sessions will be well-rehearsed and professional. Normally, too, the credibility linked to external trainers is high, and will be even higher if the trainers are part of the consultancy which worked with the organisation to facilitate the production of the values and the code.

Another feature about using external staff is that it helps to avoid impressions that 'ethically perfect' managers are being used to sermonise to others on how to conduct themselves ethically. Further, external trainers and consultants are normally in a better position to comment authoritatively on the significance of the organisation's ethics so far as its external world (customers, competitors, and suppliers) is concerned.

The three options are not mutually exclusive. Well-planned ethics training can successfully integrate positive contributions from in-house trainers, line managers, and external consultants. In-house trainers are particularly valuable as group facilitators when resolving simulation scenarios; line managers supply authority and unwittingly educate themselves while training others; external trainers or consultants add credibility, professionalism, and wider perspectives to the whole process.

As we have already seen, the internal structure of ethics training requires careful planning. Let us look first at how money can be wasted.

The training starts and finishes with low-level staff – as if they, and they alone, are responsible for the organisation's ethical stance and its ethical reputation. Many years ago, Juran showed that concern for quality is an upper-management responsibility, not a front-line focus: the same applies to corporate ethics and ethical leadership.

Ethics training is seen as a one-off event – some organisations will think that because we ran a series of workshops in 1991, then in effect we've been there, done it, and don't need to do it again.

The training itself is run on a shoe-string – so that, for example, the duration of the training is reduced to the point where it is virtually worthless, and large numbers are corralled into conference rooms in order to achieve economies of scale.

For large organisations, there may be no alterative to using large groups if the aim is to complete the ethics programme quickly. When British Airways introduced its customer-care initiative, 'Putting People First', 36,524 staff went through the initial series of events which ran continuously between November 1983 and June 1985. There was an average attendance of 140 participants at each session. Other organisations have decided to 'train' 80 or more people at a single occasion, arguing that in large groups the participants come to see themselves as part of the greater whole, to understand the effect they have on others, and to appreciate the importance of jettisoning unethical actions which damage their colleagues and the company's customers.

We regard such propositions as specious. So-called 'training' with such large groups is not training at all, but a religious revival meeting. It may

- be inspirational – but only if imaginatively led
- cause some people to suspend their disbelief – but not for long
- be cheap – but not cost-effective.

Presentations in front of conference-sized audiences will inevitably dwell on rhetoric, sweeping generalisations and emotional appeals – all very well in their place, but not much use if you're a counter clerk, a delivery driver, or a hotel receptionist, and you want to know what you're expected to *do* differently.

The training becomes propaganda – hectoring large audiences is not likely to achieve anything in the way of behavioural change. It may even be counter-productive, with individuals reacting adversely to what they perceive as an insult to their intelligence, or to implied accusations about the unethical actions which have hitherto formed a major component in their lives.

It is thought that lecturing to people is an effective method for enhancing ethical skills. If reading about a skill, or listening to someone talk about a skill, were truly good ways of improving performance, then all of us could become accomplished lovers in a fairly short time (just as long as it takes to scan *The Joy of Sex*).

The issues and examples are remote from the workplace realities – because the case-studies focus on macro-ethical dilemmas for top managers instead of the micro-ethical scenarios frequently encountered at lower levels (and examined in Chapter 4).

Whenever senior executives are asked to list the types of conflict they have experienced between their ethical beliefs and their obligations to their employers, the following categories suggest themselves:[15]

- price discrimination and unfair pricing
- giving and receiving gifts, gratuities, and bribes
- treatment of employees, especially so far as discrimination and equal opportunities are concerned
- cheating customers and dishonesty in contracts.

A very different picture emerges if we ask middle- and lower-level managers what their most important moral conflicts are, as Evans[16] has shown:

- complying with a superior's requirements when they conflict with your own code of ethics
- job demands infringing on domestic obligations
- methods employed in the competition for promotion
- avoiding or hedging responsibility.

These data indicate that those below top management largely experience role conflicts because of perceived 'pressure from above' – a view already discussed in Chapter 2.

In his recent book, Edmund Marshall[17] presents some mini-cases as part of his 'Business Ethics Game'. They supply opportunities for discussion either in their original form or in versions adapted for specific situations. See Table 7.1 for one of Marshall's ethical posers.

Table 7.1

You have discovered that one (or more) of your superiors at work is involved in a business practice which you are convinced is damaging to the long-term business interests of your organisation, if not illegal. Do you:

a. do nothing?
b. take up the issue with person(s) concerned?
c. report the matter to another senior manager?
d. report the matter anonymously to the police or to the regulatory authority if there is one?
e. seek the earliest opportunity to leave the organisation?

Individual or syndicate choices can be measured against the actions suggested by the ethical values and code of conduct, or against the general canons of ethical leadership. Other mini-cases written by Marshall cover such themes as bribery by suppliers, variable treatment of different customers, conflicts over 'professional' standards versus business objectives, and the handling of emotional relationships at work involving some threat of blackmail. The generality of the cases, as we have seen, enables them to be speedily translated into particular organisational settings.

Another source of inspiration for plausible discussion vehicles on ethical leadership is the work of Midi Berry and William Keyser.[18] One of their case-studies, though more targeted towards senior management audiences, explores the centrality of ethical values themselves (see Table 7.2).

Case-study construction is particularly problematic if training in ethical leadership is undertaken across cultural barriers, not only within a single country's multi-ethnic workforce but also across European or global operations. As Fons Trompenaars points out,[19] one of the foundations of cultural

Table 7.2

You are part of a top management group that recently developed a draft statement of corporate values. One item with which everyone seemed satisfied was 'We will conduct ourselves according to the highest standards of honesty and integrity.' The statement was shared with all managers in the company, in a series of meetings intended to stimulate discussion: reactions have varied from mild enthusiasm to cynicism. A senior accountant in your division, your direct report, with a dotted line relationship to the finance director, tells you her concerns about the way in which certain corporate accounting practices are being conducted. She says it is common knowledge in finance that the company sails close to the wind, and describes specific examples of sharp practice in which she was pressured to collude. She feels this doesn't square with the newly espoused statement on honesty and integrity. She had been wanting to speak out before, but was afraid. Now she feels, for the sake of the statement of corporate values, that people can't ignore what's going on. She anticipates that raising these issues with the finance director would be 'like talking to a brick wall'. What action will you take?

differences is a preference for universalism versus particularism. Universalism implies a commitment to what in Chapter 1 we called 'transcendental ethics', namely, behaviour which is 'good' and 'right' across the board. Particularism ('social ethics' in another guise), by contrast, allows far more credit to be given to the obligations of relationships and unique circumstances. For example, instead of assuming that there is a 'good' route always to be followed, the particularist may reason that friendship has special significance and should come first. People with particularist beliefs are much less likely to endorse abstract societal or religious codes, like the Ten Commandments, and hence are likely to encounter difficulties in accepting, endorsing and applying any organisation-wide ethical values.

Business people from particularist societies will tend to think that universalists are corrupt, and vice versa. A universalist will say, of particularists, 'They cannot be trusted because they will always help their friends', whereas a particularist, conversely, will say of universalists that 'You cannot trust them: they would not even help a friend.'

The story in Table 7.3, created by Stouffer and Toby (and used widely by Trompenaars), takes the form of a dilemma which measures universalist and particularist responses.

Table 7.3

> You are riding in a car driven by a close friend. He hits a pedestrian. You know he was going at least 35 miles per hour in an area of the city where the maximum allowed speed is 20 miles per hour. There are no witnesses. His lawyer says that if you testify under oath that he was driving only at 20 miles per hour it may save him from serious consequences. What right has your friend to expect you to protect him?
>
> a My friend has a definite right as a friend to expect me to testify to the lower figure.
> b He has some right as a friend to expect me to testify to the lower figure.
> c He has no right as a friend to expect me to testify to the lower figure.
>
> What do you think you would do in view of the obligations of a sworn witness and the obligation to your friend?
>
> d Testify that he was going at 20 miles per hour.
> e Not testify that he was going at 20 miles per hour.

Source: Fons Trompenaars, *Riding the Waves of Culture*, London, Economist Books, 1993, p. 34.

Having used this scenario among many hundreds of respondents, Trompenaars reports that North Americans and most North Europeans emerge as universalist in their approach to the problem. The proportion falls to under 70 per cent for the French and Japanese, while in Venezuela two-thirds of respondents would lie to the police to protect their friend.

The universalists' response is that as the seriousness of the accident increases, the obligation to help their friend decreases. They seem to be saying to themselves, 'The law was broken and the serious condition of the pedestrian underlines the importance of upholding the law.' This suggests that universalism is rarely used to the exclusion of particularism, but rather that it forms the first principle in the process of 'autonomous reasoning' on moral issues. In particularist cultures, however, support for the friend *increases* with the severity of the pedestrian's injuries. Their reasoning seems to be, 'My friend needs my help even more now that he is in serious trouble with the law.' Universalists regard such attitudes as corrupt: what would be the consequences if we all started to lie on behalf of those close to us?

Cultures are not invariably universalist or particularist. French and Brazilian managers, particularist when assessing the traffic accident, were conspicuously universalist – committed to truth – when the moral issue involved a subject as important as food (which is the central theme of another Trompenaars mini-case). It is also noticeable that the Japanese, particularist about the traffic accident and therefore willing to help their friend, are much less willing to help friends if to do so would require a breach of corporate confidentiality (ie, dropping hints in advance about their own company's performance or strategic intentions).

Review

As we have seen, training in ethical conduct is not a trivial issue which can be easily resolved. It requires adequate resources, skilfully deployed. Resources thoughtlessly dissipated will signal the organisation's apparent belief that problems can be solved simply by throwing money and people at them. If resources are not made available, on the other hand, then the ethical values, at best, will be only partially successful in shaping behaviour.

The Cummins experience shows what can be done through intelligent assessment of the need and a skilful application of learning psychology, without extravagant use of corporate capital. We have also pointed to the mistakes which can be made. Many of these mistakes are applicable to all forms of training, but they have special significance for training in business ethics because of the sensitive nature of the training's objectives; in particular, the need to walk a delicate tightrope between moral indoctrination on the one hand and the complete absence of any ethical restrictions on the other. The midway point is the practice of 'moral maturity', the achievable goal being the capacity to think and act ethically within the framework of the organisation's ethical values.

Our brief exploration into cultural differences is particularly relevant to global organisations seeking to establish a set of ethical values applicable to every aspect of their operations. SmithKline Beecham's 'Simply Better' values and leadership practices, and 'The Philips Way' for Philips Electronics, are intended for world-wide application as if they are global 'products' like Coca-Cola. In the event, some local variations have been essential, although the underlying models remain untouched. What has been remarkable, indeed, has been the success of the integrative process, for both these benchmark companies, in achieving assimilation for their ethical principles across multi-faceted cultural, ethnic, linguistic and even religious boundaries. The experience of such organisations suggests that much can be achieved through ethical leadership from the top coupled with systematic training and powerful two-way communication.

In our next chapter we assess the role of HR in the design, implementation and renewal of ethical values. In particular, we establish the links between training and communication, showing how the two processes must proceed in parallel and must reinforce each other if meaningful outcomes are to be accomplished.

References

1. G.C.S. Benson, 'Codes of ethics', *Journal of Business Ethics*, Vol. 8, No. 5, 1989, pp. 305–319.

2. Patrick MacLagan, 'From moral ideals to moral action: lessons for management development', *Management Education and Development*, Vol. 22, Part 1, 1991, pp. 3–14.
3. L. Kohlberg, 'Stage and sequence: the cognitive-developmental approach to socialisation', in D.A. Goslin (ed.), *Handbook of Socialisation Theory and Research*, Chicago, Rand-McNally, 1969. See also L. Kohlberg, 'Continuities in childhood and adult moral development revisited', in P.B. Baltes and K.W. Schaie (eds), *Life Span Development Psychology: Personality and Socialisation*. New York, Academic Press, 1973.
4. J. Rowan, 'Ethical issues in organisational change', in P.B. Warr, (ed.), *Personal Goals and Work Design*, Chichester, John Wiley, 1976; B. Victor and J.B. Cullen, 'The organisational bases of ethical work climates', *Administrative Science Quarterly*, Vol. 33, No. 1, 1988, pp. 101–125; R. Snell, 'Questioning the ethics of management development – a critical review', *Management Education and Development*, Vol. 17, No. 1, 1986, pp. 43–64.
5. Archie B. Carroll, 'Principles of business ethics – their role in decision-making and an initial consensus', *Management Decision*, Vol. 25, No. 8, 1990, pp. 20–24.
6. Patrick MacLagan, *op. cit.*, p. 7.
7. S.W. Gellerman, 'Why "good" managers made bad ethical choices', *Harvard Business Review*, Vol. 64, No. 4, July–August 1986, pp. 85–90.
8. Michael Hammer and James Champy, *Re-Engineering the Corporation: A manifesto for business revolution*, London, Nicholas Brealey, 1993, pp. 65–82.
9. See, for instance, 'Can ethics be taught? Harvard gives it the old college try', by John A. Byrne, *Business Week*, 6 April 1992, p. 36.
10. Jack Mahoney, *Management Education and Business Ethics*, Professional Practice Committee Discussion Paper, London, British Institute of Management, December 1991, p. 2.
11. Ronald Nelson, 'Training on ethics: Cummins Engine Company', *Journal of Management Development*, Vol. 11, No. 4, 1992, pp. 21–33.
12. Milton H. Snoeyenbos, 'Integrating ethics into the business school curriculum', *Journal of Management Development*, Vol. 11, No. 4, 1992, pp. 11–20.
13. John Akers, 'Ethics and competitiveness – putting first things first', *Sloan Management Review*, Winter 1989, pp. 69–71.

14. Kenneth Andrews, 'Ethics in practice', *Harvard Business Review*, Vol. 67, No. 5, September–October 1989, pp. 99–104.
15. S. Vitell and T.A. Festervanc, 'Business ethics: conflicts, practices and beliefs of industrial managers', *Journal of Business Ethics*, Vol. 6, 1987, pp. 111–122.
16. C.E. Evans, Appendix B to T.F. McMahon, 'Moral problems of middle management', in *Proceedings of the Catholic Theological Society of America*, Vol. 20, 1965, pp. 23–49.
17. Edmund Marshall, *Business and Society*, London, Routledge, 1993, pp. 106–111.
18. Midi Berry and William Keyser, 'Business and ethics', in Ralph Stacey, (ed.), *Strategic Thinking and the Management of Change*, London, Kogan Page, 1993, p. 147.
19. Fons Trompenaars, *Riding the Waves of Culture*, London, Economist Books, 1993, p. 31 *et seq*.

8

The Role of HR in Business Conduct

Because ethical values, vision statements and corporate codes of behaviour are often viewed as part of 'people management', human resources departments have frequently assumed primary responsibility for their development and implementation. Sometimes the HR function has easily initiated the exercise as part of its perceived role as upholder of the corporate conscience. More cynically, the motives could stem from HR's desire to increase its strategic power and influence. Some of the HR-inspired initiatives are genuinely proactive; others are pre-emptive; still others are defensive. Much depends on the culture of the organisation, the board's effectiveness in promoting change, and the internal credibility of HR

From some points of view, HR sponsorship and promotion of ethical values is logical enough. If companies need a 'conscience', they are more likely to find it in the HR office than in, say, the production or marketing suites. On the other hand, the chairman may be a perfectly adequate 'conscience' – noticeably more so than HR people in many cases. In such scenarios the HR department will be the messenger rather than the originator so far as any ethical values are concerned.

Tacit acceptance of the HR function as a repository for ethical guidance can be found in the fact that, for many organisations, employees with queries about ethical issues and the interpretation of any code of business conduct are encouraged to pursue their concerns with the personnel department. At Digital Electronics Corporation, for instance, 'Our personnel organisation, the law department, and line managers responsible for our business are available to any Digital Equipment employee with an ethics or business conduct question.'[1] In some organisations, alleged violations of the ethical values and conduct codes are channelled to HR, though admittedly this is not typical (recourse to normal management control processes is more likely).

In this chapter, we review the variety of ways in which the HR manager can be involved in setting and sustaining the ethical agenda. Our discussion refers briefly to the principal specialist functions within the HR role, but concentrates at length on communications as an essential buttress to the maintenance and promotion of ethical values. HR's perspectives have to be both inner-directed and externally-focused: inner-directed because of the need to ensure that all HR policies, procedures and systems are aligned to the ethical values, and externally-focused if HR is, so to speak, to keep its eye on ethical conduct in other parts of the organisation.

The Role of HR in Ethics

Introducing a set of ethical values will involve HR from several standpoints. We touch on them here, and they are discussed at greater length later:

Recruitment and selection – the processes themselves may have to be adapted in alignment with the ethical values, and requirements may have to be modified to ensure that newly-attracted candidates understand and accept the implications of the organisation's ethical principles.

Training and development – from induction to board level, all training and development activities (not just courses) must exemplify the ethical values. Training needs are suggested by the values, so training packages have to be designed and delivered, and performance change evaluated.

Reward strategies – if some system of performance-related pay is in operation, then measurement of performance (including the specification of performance objectives within the appraisal process) must take account of compliance with the ethical values. Care must be taken that the drive for improved performance, and pay, does not lead to ethical standards being compromised.

Performance issues – all scenarios involving employee behaviour – discipline, grievance-handling, counselling, and so forth – must be reviewed and, if necessary, modified.

Communication – HR must ensure that all employees are aware of the ethical values, the associated code of conduct, and the relevance for each of them personally.

At the same time, we believe that it is very dangerous if it appears that the issue of organisational ethics has been hijacked by HR. If the exercise is an HR initiative, its impact can be reduced or even rendered wholly ineffective. This will happen if

- HR lacks political clout
- the ethical values can be perceived as anti-commercial in spirit and/or intention because of their origins in the HR department
- the involvement of HR causes other functions or individuals to breathe a sigh of relief and take a back seat

It should already be clear from the messages conveyed elsewhere in this book, particularly Chapter 3, that our conception of ethical leadership relies upon its acceptance as a key feature of the organisation's vision and corporate strategy. If it needs saying again, then we will reinforce the point that the requirement for explicit ethical values does not just stem from the desire to treat people fairly. In addition, our argument is that ethical values (if properly designed, implemented, and reinforced) are a powerful source of competitive advantage. Treating stakeholders honourably – whether they be inside the organisation or external to it – is not just a matter of principle, but is also an *input*, a *process*, a means to an end. HR, too, if it is to add value, must be driven principally by the goal of improving the performance of people inside the organisation.

Given that ethical leadership has a strongly corporate dimension, then it has to be stimulated, owned, and promoted by the board as a whole, a point already explored in Chapter 6. That does not preclude the possibility that HR will wield considerable influence behind the scenes, especially since we might expect that HR professionals would be reasonably well informed about ethical matters. This represents another danger, namely that HR attempts to dominate the ethical high ground by acting as if it is the only part of the organisation populated by professionals who daily cope with problems of confidentiality, communication, and dilemmas about integrity.

If the ethical values are genuinely corporate, they are more likely to be linked to the achievement of strategic goals relevant to the whole organisation, and not merely by people-management principles like equal opportunities and staff development. Such principles are fine in themselves, of course, and we should not be dismissive about the HR obligation to set an example through its own professional conduct within these arenas, but they fall very short of being strategies linked to corporate outcomes.

In Jane Pickard's view,[2] HR's contribution to enhancing awareness of ethical issues can come in three forms:

- the deployment of professional expertise to develop and communicate an ethics policy and field the response to it, holding training sessions to help people think through the issues, and monitoring the policy's effectiveness – presumably with a view to proposing further improvements
- a contribution to forming corporate strategy, especially touching on vision and ethical values
- role-modelling across the organisation through its own policies and practices

It is relatively rare for HR people to be involved in the

development of explicit ethical values. We think this is a mistake, and not principally because of our own personal commitment to HR. First, the HR function is expected to identify itself with the training and communication needed at the 'making-it-happen' phase: this is much more likely to be undertaken effectively if HR has some ownership for the 'product'. Secondly, HR is already accustomed to handling the ethical issues that regularly arise in such fields as equal opportunities, recruitment, selection, training/development, performance review, discipline, and so forth. It is only a mild extension of this competence which would enable HR to contribute powerfully to more general issues of business conduct.

At various points in this book we have promoted the potential contribution of HR in prodding top management towards the production of clear ethical values and a code of conduct, in communicating across the organisation, in driving and sustaining the momentum, in training, and in developing enhancements to the ethical values in the light of internal feedback and external benchmarking. We have said much less about the application of the key ethical values and a code of conduct within the HR function itself. It is to this that we now turn. If the HR department cannot demonstrate ethical leadership, then why should anyone else?

Integrating HR policies with the ethical values

As we have said many times, all HR policies and practices must be consistent with the ethical values and the conduct code. It is beyond the scope of our enquiries to specify precisely what this means for the full range of HR corporate interventions on manpower planning, recruitment, selection, training and development, reward systems, performance management, appraisal, discipline, redundancy, retirements, employee involvement and employment relations. Instead, we shall illustrate our thesis by reference to some selected examples, preceded by a brief discussion of the place of 'ethics' and 'values' in current HR thinking, since such matters are rarely brought out into the open.

A survey of some modern texts on HR and personnel management[3] reveals virtually no references to 'ethics' or 'values' in their indexes or chapter headings. Yet employer-employee relationships are shot through with ethical implications. Should employees be expected to behave ethically, they must also be dealt with properly by their employers. To some extent the nature of the employer-employee relationship is regulated by law, but many features of these relationships go beyond the law and address issues of principle which do not lend themselves readily to firm legislative contracts.

In the previous chapter we looked at the processes of whistle-blowing: now we take the treatment of whistle-blowers themselves as a case for ethical treatment. In many recent whistle-blowing situations, the operative policy has been to dismiss the individual concerned, who has then found it virtually impossible to secure employment elsewhere. Failure to respond to the problem revealed by the whistle-blowing, but instead to punish the messenger, has a chilling effect on any internal reward system which promotes ethical business conduct. For this and other reasons, employees may interpret their working environment as a context in which it is safer not to act ethically, since to do so is more likely to generate retribution than recognition.

Even if HR's ethical stance is implicit rather than explicit, the very phrase 'human resource management' has been cited as evidence of a fundamental shift in values concerning the treatment of people in organisations. The jury is still out on such arguments. We incline to Karen Legge's view[4] that 'Undoubtedly, some changes, in some sectors of industry, have taken place in the management of the labour process and in employment relationships. This largely reflects a pragmatic response to opportunities and constraints in the present socio-politico-economic environment, rather than constituting expressions of a coherent new employment philosophy.' What undoubtedly has occurred is a move away from 'soft' normative models of HRM and towards 'harder' perspectives.[5]

The 'hard' model stresses the need for a close integration between HR policies, systems and activities with the organisation's strategic direction. In essence, the 'hard' model emphasises (in Storey's words) the 'quantitative, calculative and business strategic aspects of managing the headcount resource in as "rational" a way as for any other economic factor'.[6] By contrast, the 'soft' HRM model, while still requiring HR policies to be integrated with corporate objectives, suggests the treatment of employees as valued assets – as a source of competitive advantage for the organisation through their commitment, adaptability, and high quality. Employees, according to this view, are proactive rather than passive inputs into the production of work-outputs. Because employees are capable of development, the HRM focus should be on generating commitment on the grounds that it will yield better economic performance for the organisation.

If the 'hard' approach concentrated on human *resource management*, the 'soft' model relies upon *human resource* management. It is mistaken, in our view, to think that the 'hard' and 'soft' frameworks are conceptually polarised. For the organisation pursuing a strategy of high value-added growth, then treating its employees as resourceful humans to be developed by humanistic policies makes good business sense. This is all very well, but, as Legge points out, what of the organisation which is competing in a labour-intensive, high-volume, low-cost industry, generating profits through increasing market share by cost leadership? For such organisations, the HR policies likely to be seen to be most appropriate, in order to contribute to strategic objectives, will probably treat employees as a variable input and as a cost to be minimised. Such treatment is a far cry from the aspirations of ethical leadership, yet is understandable for companies more interested in the fundamentals of surviving than in advancing the cause of some (what seem to them to be) moral abstractions unrelated to the 'real' world.

What these points demonstrate is that strategic management itself is riddled with value-judgements. Similarly, HR policies and HR practitioners (given that they are human beings) are similarly weighed down with philosophical baggage, more commonly leaning towards the 'soft' HR perspective than the 'hard' one. In our view this is because people are frequently attracted into HR for the wrong reasons: because of some vague 'liking for people' or a wish to work with people which they believe can only be fulfilled in an HR role.[7]

For many organisations, the distinction between 'hard' and 'soft' HRM frameworks must seem arid and theoretical. It is by no means the case that only 'soft' organisations will have ethical values and conduct codes, though, if they do, they would justify such processes by reference to some 'soft' philosophical assumptions about people-potential and commitment. Where 'hard' organisations – like Dixons, SmithKline Beecham, and Cadbury-Schweppes – have ethical values and conduct codes, their rationale will characteristically be different, founded on the possibility of business and competitive advantage. There is no reason to suppose that operationally the justification for ethical values makes any difference to the actual results. On the other hand, the 'soft' or 'hard' HRM culture does influence the extent to which values and codes are prescriptive rather than proscriptive, positive rather than negative.

For instance, Walter Manley's book on business conduct[8] has a section showing examples of codes of conduct relating to 'The Firm's Commitment to its Employees and Employee Relations'. Under this heading there are entries specifying such companies as Alcan, Dixons, ICL, George Wimpey, TI Group, Scott Bader, Abbey Life, Burmah Oil, Coats-Viyella, Ciba-Geigy, United Biscuits, the John Lewis Partnership, and Digital. Here is the Dixons contribution in full:

> Employees are not normally allowed to leave their normal place of work during working hours or to receive visitors or receive or make private telephone calls without the

> permission of their Manager or Supervisor. At certain
> locations, pay phones are installed for use by employees.

Part of the Abbey Life material, by contrast, reads as
follows:

> Abbey recognises that employees and the managers
> responsible for them should maintain relationships based
> on mutual respect and recognition of each other's rights
> and obligations. The employees' rights are:
>
> (1) to contribute to decisions likely to affect them indi-
>   vidually
> (2) to know what is expected of them and how they are
>   meeting this expectation
> (3) to have their aspirations considered
> (4) to feel that they are fairly treated.
>
> Manager's rights are:
>
> (1) to organise and direct employees towards objectives
> (2) to expect rules and standards to be upheld
> (3) to expect enthusiasm, co-operation and commitment.

If the Dixons tone appears to be 'hard', the inference may be
misleading, but it may be helpful to refer to Karen Legge's
comments[9] about the HR policies likely to be pursued by
organisations which are competing in a labour-intensive, high-
volume, low-cost industry, generating profits through increasing market share by cost leadership. Dixons fulfils most of
these criteria. Abbey Life's approach, by contrast, seems to be
'soft' but in reality is just as focused on business outcomes.

Organisations choose to achieve their business goals in
differing ways, and the HR implications will therefore be
different as well. HR policies and practices may be critically
evaluated against the extent to which they will enable predeter-
mined corporate goals to be attained – in other words, whether
they are suitable 'means' for a given 'end' – but to evaluate
them against the criteria of ethical leadership, though permiss-
ible, is far more problematic. If we find ourselves more
comfortable with the underlying messages in Abbey Life's

code than with the Dixons approach, maybe that says more
about us than about them.

Employee training and development

The principles of ethical leadership, whether performed
against a 'hard' or 'soft' set of HRM assumptions, nonetheless
agree that the abilities and skills of staff should be utilised to
the greatest possible extent. However, staff performance and
growth are not normally viewed as benefits in themselves so far
as the organisation is concerned. As Abbey Life expresses it:

> The intention is to match as far as possible the developing
> competence and aspirations of staff to the needs of the
> business so that employees share in the company's success.

Abbey Life spells out the belief that 'individuals should bear
the primary responsibility for their own career development by
keeping up-to-date and acquiring the skills and experience
needed for growth. The company's role will be to identify
potential and help fulfil it.' Abbey Life is enlightened enough
to visualise possibilities – especially in today's delayered
hierarchies – of frustrations when employees reach the limit of
their career development.

> This will be discussed openly and honestly to avoid
> dissatisfaction and frustration from unrealistic ambitions.
> We also appreciate that in these circumstances some staff
> may wish to develop alternative careers outside Abbey
> and we will seek to facilitate such moves where it is
> compatible with our business needs.

Similarly, but even more vigorously, ICL stresses that it is a
'people company'.[10]

> The company will constantly aim to provide you with
> responsibilities and objectives which measure up to your
> abilities and ambitions – and ideally stretch them a little

too. The company is determined to satisfy your need for personal growth and job satisfaction, and to create the supportive environment which enables you to achieve them.

However, individuals have to make a good deal of the running. The most rewarding development is self-development and employees are expected to help themselves by pushing their managers for guidance, for opportunities, for appropriate formal training, and for new kinds of work experience.

Discipline and disciplinary regulations

Ethical values and corporate codes of conduct differ enormously in terms of whether they say anything at all about discipline and the nature of those offences which would justify disciplinary action, whether they seek to specify the offences and the penalties, and the amount of space allocated to such considerations. Scott Bader merely indicates that 'management by consent rather than coercion is an appropriate style for the company',[11] whereas organisations in such fields as financial services will elaborate at length about offences involving conflicts of interest. Perhaps IBM's approach says all that is necessary while indicating that the responsibility lies principally with the employee to make an intelligent judgement:

> Your private life is very much your own. Still, a conflict of interest may arise if you engage in any activities or advance any personal interests at the expense of IBM's interests. It's up to you to avoid situations in which your loyalty may become divided.[12]

Anti-discrimination and equal opportunity

Discrimination is illegal under the Race Relations Act of 1976 and the Employment Acts of 1982 and 1985. It is also unprofitable if it means that the organisation deprives itself of significant sources of potential talent, ability, knowledge, and skill. One might hope that the case against discrimination had been made to the point where it is now a dead issue. Unfortunately this is not the case. Unethical organisations, managers, and employees can still harass employees or implement prejudicial pay and reward systems, by passing over people for otherwise justified promotions, by promoting people to unwanted positions, or by use of a 'glass ceiling' invisibly separating some sectors of the workforce from others in terms of recruitment, communication, transfer and pro-motability.

All statements of ethical values will say something about people being treated as individuals without regard for sex, race, ethnic origin, religion, physical disability, and so forth. Some codes of conduct will elaborate on these principles at great length, making it clear not only that discrimination of any type will not be tolerated, but also that there are severe sanctions involved. In the case of equal opportunity, too, it is often recognised that 'fair dealing' for employees should be extended to suppliers, agents, potential employees, and con-tractors.

HR's role in communicating the ethical values

Even though the organisation may be committed to ethical leadership, the actual effectiveness of the whole process depends on constructing implementation mechanisms which are vigorous, robust and inexorable. Training (discussed at length in Chapter 7) is one key part of these mechanisms; communication is another. We cannot reasonably expect that everyone will read, accept, and absorb messages about ethics simply because they are widely available and trumpeted from the roof-tops. Some will not read or listen to the messages in the first place; some will think it does not apply to them; some will misunderstand the message, wilfully or otherwise; some will reject it; only a few will take it on board, probably complaining about the fact that it's taken so long to bring the ethical issue to the surface.

So communicating the ethical values and the code of conduct is going to be hard work. It requires unremitting effort, skilled presentation, and single-minded unity of content and approach. HR will play a crucial part in designing the communication processes, making them happen, and measuring the results. In the context of this book we can only outline some of the principles involved.

Surprisingly enough, the first thing to do is actually to distribute copies of the ethical values and the code of conduct. Some organisations seem to regard such documents as commercially confidential, so their circulation is limited to top managers and senior executives. We even encountered a company recently which told its customers and clients about its newly-drafted mission statement, but failed to say anything to its own employees – which surely says something about the purposes behind the mission statement and the seriousness of the company's commitment to it.

A wide distribution of the ethical values, accompanied at the outset by a readily-understandable message from the CEO, is preferable for five obvious reasons:

- Particularly if the organisation is in a service industry, then maintenance of the ethical values is critically dependent on 'moments of truth' between front-line employees and customers. If front-line employees are not given guidance about the values and, even more, the code of conduct, then there is no likelihood whatever that their behaviour will change.
- Wide availability of ethical values and conduct code material gives notice to everyone that the concept is not frivolous.
- Incorporation of the ethical values and the code in material sent to customers and suppliers will help to show that the organisation has an external, customer-facing focus. If knowledge about the ethical values raises the expectations of customers and suppliers about the way they will be treated, then their propensity to give feedback to the organisation

will be increased. Experience suggests, too, that such feedback tends to be more positive and constructive than before
– in other words, it is not solely about discrepancies between
the ideals and the action.

- If the organisation wishes to enlist all its employees in a
  common cause, it cannot do so if knowledge about the
  ethical values is restricted to a select few.
- Regular and systematic repetition of the ethical values helps
  gradually to embed them. The J Bibby policy document
  encapsulating the company's 'Core Values' is reproduced in
  the annual report and accounts, the annual employee report,
  and the quarterly newsletter. BT highlights its values
  through internal newspaper articles, plus laminated cards
  issued to all employees; at Peugeot Talbot, managers display
  framed copies of the Company Charter.

Other distribution techniques include sending a copy of the
ethical values material to all employees through the post;
incorporating the ethical values into all policy and procedure
manuals; and making the ethical values available within the
computer network (as IBM does), especially for employees
who have dealings with outside parties. None of these
approaches is mutually exclusive.

If ethical values and an explicit code of conduct are being
introduced for the first time, then the manner of communicating is especially critical. A message from the CEO assists in
conveying the significance of the exercise; it is reinforced when
the CEO attends launch events. Criteria for the CEO's
message are

Why some ethical values are being put together (or modified,
if an earlier version is already in existence). It is better to use
positive arguments about the benefits of behaving as a responsible member of society, rather than crude materialistic suggestions about business advantage. Not only are such suggestions
likely to be inconsistent with the tone of the ethical values, but
their inclusion can cause people to think that the whole thing

is nothing more than a cynical PR adventure. For similar reasons, it is equally desirable to avoid any impression that the values are merely a response to legislative, regulatory or other external threats.

Generalised references to the fact that the (new) ethical values build on the organisation's existing standards and principles. This will avoid any impression of indirect accusations that anyone has been unethical in the past.

Clear statements about the prohibition on all unethical or illegal actions, plus the measures available to ensure that such prohibitions are sustained.

Possibly some rhetorical questions (along the lines of the 'Private Eye Test' mentioned in Chapter 2) which employees should ask themselves if ever contemplating some action (or inaction) which the organisation would regard as unethical:

- 'Would I be willing to tell my family about the action that I am contemplating, or that I am being asked to take?'
- 'Would I feel any misgivings if society knew of the action I am contemplating?'
- 'Would it be a problem for me if my actions were to be published in the company magazine or newspaper?'

In gaining acceptance for ethical leadership, the organisation must rely on a trusting, supportive and open system of communications – a goal which is often enshrined within the ethical values themselves. If the environment is suspicious and defensive, employees will suppress their opinions and feelings.

People do not respond to reality, but rather to their perceptions of reality. It is not enough to state that the organisation encourages open communication. If such statements do not coincide with employee impressions, then it will take time for new patterns to emerge and for the inhibitions based on fear to be replaced by a willingness to speak freely.

As with all communication, the distribution of the ethical values must start from where employees are, not from where we would like them to be. We have to work with their existing attitudes, preconceptions, beliefs, and prejudices. Effective communication of the ethical values and any associated code of conduct requires

- its translation into an employee-meaningful frame of reference
- the use of images and memorable word pictures
- examples that people can readily understand
- cross-reference to traditional values and common beliefs
- understanding the audience and the need to modify the words to accommodate multiple audiences, especially in large, geographically diversified or global organisations
- repeating the message often and in different ways, so that 'repetition' does not slide into 'repetitiveness'
- being positive and upbeat about the benefits, rather than stressing the dangers and the risks
- involving the audience in the communication process
- the display of personal conviction by all those crucially involved.

Conclusion

In this chapter we have touched on some of the areas in which the HR function can direct, influence or operationalise the organisation's ethical values and code of conduct. There are many other fields in which such issues are relevant in order to enhance the objectivity and fairness which should be underpinning principles for appraisal and performance management. Handling redundancies, too, presents once again the dilemma previously linked to training and development, namely the degree of precedence to be accorded to the needs of the individual as opposed to the requirements of the organisation. Even if priorities can be agreed, there are bound to be instances where managers get it wrong.

Responsible organisations will have the interests of their employees in mind, whether their HR perspective is 'hard' or 'soft' in Storey's terms. Further, organisations must be constantly alert to the appearance of new issues. Discrimination and equal opportunity were focal points in the 1970s and 1980s; today's concerns will concentrate not only the whole repertoire of the organisation's ethical face, but also some specific themes like alcohol and drug abuse. National Westminster Bank's code of conduct, for example, embodies the principle that dependence on alcohol and drugs is an illness which can respond to appropriate treatment. This makes sense from a humanitarian perspective; it also makes sense commercially. A programme of treatment can be particularly cost-effective when measured against the alternative cost of replacing employees terminated for alcohol and drug abuse.

The case of alcohol and drug abuse also illustrates the point, made over and over again in this book, that having a set of ethical values, buttressed by a code of conduct, is not sufficient to facilitate change and the appropriate behaviour patterns. Just as a whistle-blower's charter will not by itself stop people from blowing whistles, so a range of policies to counter alcohol and drug abuse relies on the preparedness of employees to admit that they have a problem.

Voluntary commitment, and therefore a gradually accelerating pattern of behaviour change, depends on determined HR initiatives and role-modelling:

- HR must work with senior management to ensure that the ethical values are clear and supportive, rather than ambiguous and judgemental.
- HR must secure adequate resources sufficiently to enable the conduct guidelines to be implemented. These 'resources' include political support from the top.

- HR must promote the environment of trust necessary before employees will come forward with problems of a personal (alcohol, drug abuse, and so forth) or corporate (whistle-blowing) nature.
- HR must guarantee that all cases are managed construct-ively and positively, especially those at the outset of the exercise, so that credibility is reinforced and cynicism is silenced.

References

1. Walter W. Manley II, *The Handbook of Good Business Practice*, London, Routledge, 1992, p. 48.
2. Jane Pickard, 'Prepare to make a moral judgement', *People Management*, 4 May 1955, pp. 22–25.
3. See, for instance; John Storey, ed., *Human Resource Management – A critical text*, London; Routledge, 1995; Christopher Molander and Jonathan Winterton, *Managing Human Resources*, London; Routledge, 1994; Keith Sisson, ed., *Personal Management*, Oxford; Basil Blackwell, 2nd edition, 1994; Barry Cushway, *Human Resource Management*, London; Kogan Page, 1994; Jane Weightman, *Managing Human Resources*, London; IPD, 23nd edition, 1993.
4. Karen Legge, 'HRM: rhetoric, reality and hidden agendas' in John Storey, (ed.), *Human Resource Management – A critical text*, London, Routledge, 1995, pp. 33–62.
5. The distinction between 'hard' and 'soft' normative models for HRM was discussed in John Storey, 'Developments in the management of human resources: an interim report', *Warwick Papers in Industrial Relations No 17*, University of Warwick, School of Industrial and Business Studies, 1987.
6. John Storey, *op. cit.*, 1987, p. 6.
7. One of the authors of this book used regularly to interview applicants for a full-time postgraduate diploma in personnel management course. When asked why they wanted to enter personnel management, the applicants would frequently mutter something about wanting to 'work with people'. The inter-viewer's follow-up question – 'Have you considered a career in embalming?' – seldom went down well, despite the fact that

embalming is (one supposes) a satisfyingly 'hands-on' way of working with people.

8. The material relating to Dixons and Abbey Life has been abstracted from Walter W. Manley II, *op. cit.*, pp. 164–165.
9. Karen Legge, *op. cit.*, p. 36.
10. Walter W. Manley II, *op. cit.*, p. 167.
11. Walter W. Manley II, *op. cit.*, p. 169.
12. Walter W. Manley II, *op.cit.*, p. 179.

9

■■ Ethical Leadership and Strategic
Choice

Introduction

In earlier chapters we have argued the case strongly about the benefits to be gained from a debate on both macro-ethical and micro-ethical dimensions of corporate behaviour, leading to the articulation of a focused, coherent framework for ethical leadership throughout the organisation. Our chapters on implementation, training and the role of the HR function have explored some of the guidelines and pitfalls likely to be encountered when turning concepts into meaningful reality. Now we turn to another key issue: the need to ensure that ethical leadership is fully integrated with the vision, employee values, and the organisation's strategic direction. Above all, we concern ourselves here with alignment between ethical leadership and corporate strategy, because without such alignment, ethical leadership will surely fail.

Initially, this chapter investigates the significance of ethical leadership against the background of life-cycle theory. We believe that even when ethical leadership's profile has begun to subside – itself a long way off – then the concepts will remain powerful. For many organisations, 'total quality' has become a taken-for-granted opportunity for competitive advantage, an automatic and internalised feature of employee behaviour, driving continuous improvement without the necessity for propaganda reinforcement; ethical leadership will eventually become second nature, too.

Thinking about strategy means preparing for change; change in turn implies leadership; leadership involves ethical choices in two principal spheres:

Outcomes – the strategic goals selected from the range of options regarded as available; and

178

Process – the methods by which the strategic goals will be pursued, and the leadership styles to be displayed.

Informing these ethical choices will be the values of ethical leadership. For this reason we examine the significance of managerial values in each of six main categories:

- values towards the world
- values towards humanity
- values towards employees
- values towards owners
- values towards customers
- the values of managers themselves.

Ethical leadership is increasingly acknowledged to be a crucial driver for strategic advantage. We look first at the rationale for this view, using life-cycle theory as our departure point.

Ethical leadership and life-cycle theory

Ethical leadership is relevant today – and will be relevant for some considerable time to come – because it reflects the higher aspirations of a post-industrial society, the increasing ethical expectations of customers, and the priorities of articulate employees. As we have argued before, ethical leadership is also an alternative route to competitive advantage, precisely because it is so closely aligned with – and even slightly ahead of – consumer criteria.

However, we can see a possible relationship between interest in business ethics and ethical leadership, on the one hand, and life-cycle theory on the other.

From the vantage point of 1995, 'business ethics' and ethical leadership are in the birth phase, whose features include 'the founder or guru who first thinks of the idea, conceptualises it, and publishes a seminal book'.[1] So far there have been several books and articles on ethical leadership, but none particularly seminal and certainly none to rank with Hammer and Champy on business process re-engineering or Peters and Waterman on the 1980s notion of 'excellence'. So, as we write, the momentum of literary interest in ethical leadership is still gathering pace.

Figure 9.1
A speculative ideas life-cycle

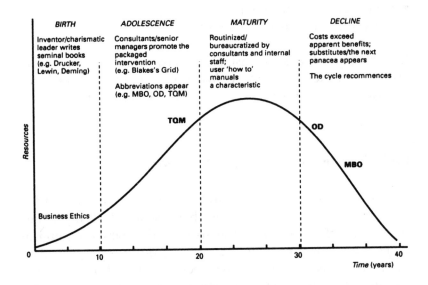

Source: J. Gill and S. Whittle, 'Management by panacea: accounting for transience', in *Journal of Management Studies*, Vol. 30, No. 2, March 1993, p. 289.

The next phase is a period of rapid growth as consultants start to develop material which will be attractive to managers. This may include one or more TLAs (three-letter-acronyms), brand names, user manuals, and diligent attempts to establish product differentiation between competing consultancies. This stage has already begun and has been further stimulated by the first report of the Nolan Committee: news items and articles about business ethics feature regularly in *Management Today*, *People Management*, and *Consult* (the periodical produced for members of the Institute of Management Consultants). In the May/June 1995 issue of *Consult*, for example, it was announced that the IMC was investigating the possibility of setting up a confidential 'ethics hotline' for its members, and also that a leading IMC member was about to publish a paper, provisionally entitled *Rewriting the Unwritten Contract*, to explain 'why Britain needs a value system', presumably to address the kind of macro-ethical issues examined in Chapter 3. Interestingly, the consultant concerned claims that 'politicians, such as Labour's Gordon Brown, are helping to give ethics a higher profile and therefore there will be a lot of work available for management consultants specialising in this field.' She helpfully warns that 'There are a lot of unqualified charlatans out there who will see it purely as a money-making opportunity, so potential clients will have to be cautious.' Less helpfully, the factors distinguishing the 'unqualified charlatans' are not specified or listed – perhaps because to spell them out would be unethical![2]

'Maturity' in the ideas life-cycle is characterised by the routinisation of material and its mechanistic reproduction. Organisations adopt ready-made, off-the-shelf 'solutions' without real commitment, but from fear of being left behind. This kind of 'me-tooism' characteristic of defensive marketing is already a noticeable feature of TQM adoption in some organisations. Hodgson's comment, in a discussion of Deming's 'road to quality', is worth reproducing because, with suitable word changes, it could easily be viewed as a warning about what can go wrong as the issue of ethical leadership takes off:[3]

> Is the quality revolution really starting here, or are we just witnessing yet another star rising in the British management firmament – shortly to join its predecessors out of sight and out of fashion? Taking the British picture as a whole, the odds seem to be on the latter. Not because people won't work hard for quality but because we will

end up trying to install the techniques of quality management and not understanding it.

Decline then sets in as a result of spreading disillusionment.
As Gill and Whittle[4] put it, 'The package becomes rigidified,
costs exceed benefits, the novelty wears off, and substitutes
appear on the scene which themselves in turn go through the
same cycle.' They could have added, with equal cynicism, that
some of the newer substitutes are simply the old ideas repack-
aged: 'empowerment' being a 1990s version of 'job enrich-
ment', which itself was a 1960s approach to 'delegation'.

In our view, the 'panacea' or 'ideas' life-cycle concept has
merit. Very few ideas last for very long without being jetti-
soned altogether or adapted, in some instances almost beyond
recognition. However, it has dangers if swallowed whole:

- The duration – or life-expectancy – of any single idea cannot
  be estimated with any confidence. Gill and Whittle tentat-
  ively suggest 40 years, yet some ideas fizzle out far more
  rapidly while others display remarkable persistence. Since
  Gill and Whittle do not reveal the reasoning behind their 40-
  year cycle, we are entitled to assume that it may be
  something to do with the fact that in the UK the average life-
  expectancy of a commercial enterprise is also 40 years.

- On the other hand, some organisations survive for centuries
  – as do some ideas, like Christianity. Even in our allegedly
  turbulent world, the average age of the top 20 grocery
  brands in the UK is 56 years.[5] The key to the continued
  success of these 'old' brands and of such 'old' ideas as
  Christianity is the fact that they never stand still: the brands
  and the ideas enjoy continual development and progress,
  essential to sustain 'consumer' interest and loyalty. So there
  is no inevitability about the belief that management ideas
  are always transient.

- The fact that an idea ceases to attract substantial publicity –
  through articles, books, media exposure, and consultancy
  promotion – does not mean that the idea has moved beyond
  its sell-by date. In the case of quality and TQM, a lower

profile just as plausibly means that a 'quality culture' has become so deeply embedded in the organisation that it is taken for granted. Quality products and services emerge naturally; continuous improvement happens automatically; change is the norm rather than the exception.

- Even if a particular idea is ultimately doomed to eclipse, it can't safely be ignored while it is in the ascendant. To be left behind when some source of competitive advantage presents itself – like TQM – is as foolish as uncritical adoption of every novelty that comes along. There is benefit in being a pioneer; ultimately, the rationale for 'late adopters' is the defensive requirement to keep pace with market leaders. That rationale may not be healthy because it is negative rather than positive, but it is convincingly preferable to the inaction which leads to competitive *dis*advantage. No organisation can afford to stand still: its competitive advantage can easily become a disadvantage if it becomes complacent, believing that the ultimate panacea has been found and that no further improvement is either necessary or possible. We need to look no further than the 'if-it-ain't-broke-don't-fix-it' strategic mentality of Marks & Spencer, in relation to customer care, to see self-satisfied insularity at work.

So what does the ideas life-cycle mean for ethical leadership? Certainly we do not claim that ethical leadership is a new idea, even if the phrase is new. Unarguably, business ethics is a big idea whose time has come. The timing is partly a consequence of adverse publicity about corporate greed and commercial cynicism; partly, too, a product of the realisation that business ethics is good business. For some organisations, conscious adoption of an ethical stance arises from instrumental bandwagon-jumping rather than from inner conviction. It will take some time before the bandwagon-jumpers are exposed by analysis of the discrepancies between their high-sounding words and the unchanging nature of their actions. Once such contrasts are revealed, the organisations will claim that trying to be ethical was actually a waste of time, effort, and resources. They will conveniently ignore the reality that they had never actually been ethical at all. Indeed, by hypocritically promoting some ethical values and a code of conduct which bear no relationship to the behaviour patterns condoned, encouraged, and rewarded, such organisations have actually become more unethical than they were before.

The only worthwhile way forward, as we have argued throughout this book, is for organisations to espouse ethical leadership in spirit, word and deed. This has to be a conspicuous process. In Chapters 6 and 7, in particular, we indicated that essential ingredients include deliberate role-modelling from the top, publicity and communications, training, modification of HR systems (especially recruitment, promotion and appraisal), and compliance/monitoring procedures. Once the ethical values and the code of conduct become embedded, the issue of ethical conduct can be allowed to recede into the background – much as 'quality' has been allowed to do in companies where quality has been established as second nature.

There is much that remains to be done. Although increasing numbers of senior managers show a great deal of interest in ethical leadership – and a few have done something about it – there are many companies which remain untouched. Even where progress has been made, it has been haphazard – as one might expect when something is introduced experimentally or as a pilot project. As the pioneers move ahead, the momentum will accelerate among those organisations which are still waiting on the sidelines, and which can learn from the lessons acquired – sometimes painfully – from those that have gone before. Once again, we must stress that deriving benefits of any kind from ethical leadership – made flesh through ethical values and a code of conduct – will only happen *if words and deeds are integrated*. Dissonance generates disillusionment, cynicism and alienation. Worse, it encourages short-term calculative responses conveying no ethical consistency at all but focusing on such 'values' as personal survival, political ascendancy, and tactical teamwork.

Integrating values, vision, ethics and strategy

Ethical issues have always been an essential component in business, but in the past were relegated to the fringes. As we saw in Chapter 1, some well-publicised cases of individual fraud, and public perceptions about corporate greed, have altered the picture. It is now much more acceptable to assume that the search for excellence and the search for ethics amount to much the same thing.

Ethics, values and the strategic dimension

The powerful link between ethical leadership and corporate strategy is reinforced in the report produced by the Management Counsel service of the Digital Equipment Company under the guidance of John Humble.[6] The report examines data from 429 UK companies, including industrial and consumer-goods manufacturing, banking and financial services, and distribution. Within the survey, corporate values were defined as

> the relatively few important beliefs which are widely held to be crucial for the success of a given organisation; those beliefs and convictions which substantially drive the behaviour of people in an organisation.

Key points from the study include:

- 80 per cent of the sample already had written value statements
- 89 per cent of the sample expected 'values' to be more important for organisational success in the future
- 82 per cent believed that properly-implemented [sic] values contribute to profitability.

Respondent priorities over the themes to be included in ethical value statements again indicate the connections between macro-ethics and strategic choice. The five most frequently mentioned issues, with specimen value statements attached, were:

- *People* – 'We believe our staff represent a crucial asset for our success.'
- *Competitiveness* – 'We are committed to providing our customers with quality and service which beats the competition.'
- *Customers* – 'We are totally dedicated to providing our customers with service that meets their needs.'
- *Quality* – 'We are committed to delivering goods and services which meet the highest objective standards.'
- *Productivity* – 'We must constantly increase the productivity of every resource in the organisation.'

The two lowest priorities were social responsibility and profitability. Very few companies were prepared to make statements such as 'We believe that short-term profit is essential for our survival.'

While the 429 organisations contributing to the Digital research were prepared to offer views about the current and future place of ethical leadership in business affairs, it remains true that most companies do not think about strategy and ethical values in an integrated way. The question seems to be whether there is competitive advantage to be gained, or a moral imperative to be fulfilled, from devoting prior thought to the issues and seeking to arrive at an ethical view through the strategic thinking process – but with the ethical assumptions left implicit rather than openly addressed.

Much depends on management's perspective (ie, management's *values*) on the role and purpose of organisations. If an organisation is seen as simply a rational entity set up in order to pursue the attainment of declared goals, then thinking about ethics and values is only appropriate in so far as ethical principles may affect the *achievement* of whatever goals the organisation has selected. Even this stance underplays the fact that ethical considerations may have influenced the choice of the *goals* themselves. When leaders of an organisation start talking about strategy, it is reasonable to assume that they want to see outcomes which are different from those being currently pursued. The ability to see a need for change, and the ability to make it happen, are central to all forms of leadership. Leadership, therefore, is central to strategic thinking and strategic thinking entails ethical choice, by intent or default. Leadership also involves ethical choices in the selection of one leadership style rather than another, and in the leadership processes employed.

According to Dave Francis,[7] it is strategically important for managers to clarify their values within six 'domains' (see Figure 9.2). These can be listed as:

Figure 9.2
The six value domains of top managers

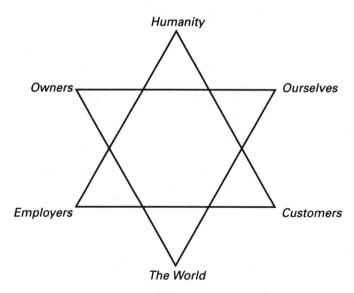

Source: Dave Francis, *Step-by-Step Competitive Strategy*, London, Routledge, 1994, p. 105.

- values towards the world
- values towards humanity
- values to employees
- values to owners
- values towards customers
- values towards ourselves (the managers).

So significant is this framework that we need to examine its implications at some length.

Values towards the world

Francis claims that 'For anyone with a conscience there seems no alternative but [to] adopt the principle that everyone with resources to dispense needs to play a part in healing our world damaged by the excesses of mankind in the twentieth century.'[8] Nobody need be in any doubt, then, about where Francis stands so far as environmental priorities are concerned.

It is legitimate for organisations to be concerned about their impact on the environment solely because they believe this concern to be ethically correct. However, some organisations will be anxious about environmental issues for more defensive reasons. They are subject to the critical attention of SIF groups like Greenpeace and Friends of the Earth. Like Shell, with its plans for disposing of the Brent Spar oil-rig, they may already have succumbed to these pressures. They may believe that their 'customers' are increasingly activated by environmental matters. If so, a tangible display of environmentalism makes good marketing sense (though having little to do with ethics). In Chapter 2 we briefly identified some of the questions about environmental issues which managers are forced to address, whether they like it or not.

The issue of organic food products illustrates the tussle between God and Mammon. When CWS Agriculture, the Co-op's farming division, embarked on its organic farming experiments in 1989, they were responding strategically to increasing concerns among pressure groups over the impact of agro-chemicals on food and the countryside. CWS Agriculture may be Britain's biggest single farmer, tending 50,000 acres in 27 locations, but even by 'cutting out the middle-man' and selling its organic produce direct to consumers, it could not make ends meet and in May 1995 eventually threw in the towel.[9] While organic produce may be attractive – apart from its dowdy appearance in shops and supermarkets alongside 'conventional' fruit and vegetables – it has not generated enough demand to make it a success, even in a (supposedly) environmentally and health-conscious age. Marks & Spencer had already abandoned organic produce, although other retailers like Sainsbury and Safeway continue to sell it for their minority of 'green' customers, and also because they believe it to be good for their image.

The regrettable reality is that many companies have paid too much attention to what customers *say* instead of simply measuring what they *do*. Seventy per cent of people are deeply concerned about the environment, but only about 11 per cent buy organic food regularly and are therefore willing to put their money where their mouth is. Organisations should heed Nishikawa's observation[10] that 'Customers are most sincere when spending rather than talking' if they wish to avoid expensive mistakes like believing that customer words are directly linked to customer behaviour.

So strategic 'values towards the world' may be ethically-driven or, more commonly, marketing-led. Once marketing becomes involved, differences between substance and reality become noticeable. Perceptive customers, or trading standards officers, observe the evasions in product labelling and the optimism of claims about benefits. Several critics have commented on Body Shop's mission to become 'the most honest cosmetic company around' (in Anita Roddick's words). If the Roddicks are single-mindedly committed to selling cosmetics and skin-care products which are natural and kind to the environment – and just happen to have hit upon a product/service package which has been hugely profitable – this does not stop some observers from speculating about the degree to which the Roddicks are ethical paragons or simply brilliant marketers. It makes a difference. If they are ethical paragons, then their success is fortuitous but welcome and somehow forgivable; if they are nothing more than brilliant marketers, then their operation is more likely to be seen as cynical, manipulative and exploitative.

Values to humanity

Awareness of the human purposes behind organisations – if articulated into a coherent, intelligible and meaningful vision – can be a source of inspiration and a dominating principle for action, as we saw in Chapter 3. At the same time, mobilising these human purposes is not inconsistent with making money. Francis may have a point when he argues that 'a myopic focus on profit is dangerous because it shifts attention from the customer to the accountant: then greed replaces prudence and short-termism elbows out commitment',[11] but in our judgement he over-states the case. In Chapter 2 we suggested that the issue is not the need to make a choice between profits *or* ethical leadership, but rather the necessity to achieve profits *through* ethical leadership. Profit, in reality, is the benefit which the organisation enjoys for providing added-value to its customers at a sustainable cost. From this standpoint, profit is a cost of staying in business.

Perhaps the clearest illustration of the ability to integrate profitability with ethical leadership is the philosophy of Konosuke Matsushita. In the 1930s he described profit as a vote of confidence from society that what is offered by the firm is valued. Failure to make profits, in his opinion, justifies corporate death because the organisation has become a waste of resources to society. Thinking in this apparently ruthless fashion, however, did not stop Matsushita from producing seven 'spiritual values' for his company – values which have a distinctively Japanese flavour but which supply a set of powerful principles underpinning the ethical leadership practised within the Matsushita organisation:

- national service through industry
- fairness
- harmony and co-operation
- struggle for betterment
- courtesy and humility
- adjustment and assimilation
- gratitude.

Values to employees

Some writers – invariably academics producing material in a spirit of disinterested detachment – have complained about the apparent hypocrisy displayed by organisations which, on the one hand, extol the virtues of a strong corporate culture while, on the other hand, claiming to respect people as individuals. Willmott, for instance, argues that organisations can create the impression of respecting individuals 'by establishing a few core values . . . [and thereby] minimising the bewildering, anxiety-laden experience of having to cope with an excess of autonomy. A strong culture, like a strong leader, is deemed to provide each employee with the security of the "sacred canopy".'[12]

Those who advocate the strengthening of corporate cultures, therefore, extend the promise of developing an environment in which employees enjoy the security of a system of beliefs – codified through ethical values – within which they can exercise severely restricted degrees of personal freedom. Willmott goes on:[13]

> In effect, corporate culture programmes are designed to deny or frustrate the development of conditions in which critical reflection is fostered. They commend the homogenization of norms and values within organisations. Employees are selected and promoted on the basis of their

(perceived) acceptance of, or receptivity to, the core
values. More generally, employees are repeatedly urged
and rewarded for suspending attachments to ideas and
norms that do not confirm and reinforce the authority of
the core values. *Cultural diversity is dissolved in the acid
bath of the core corporate values.* Those who kick against
monoculture are 'moved sideways' or they are expelled
[our emphasis].

Undoubtedly Willmott's arguments are not without justification, especially in organisations where published announcements about the value placed on people as 'our greatest asset'
are viewed with weary disbelief.[14] For such organisations, the
creation of ethical values will generate not a gain in commitment, but an unwelcome loss of credibility. Instead of a deep
identification with the values there will be selective, calculative
compliance, a 'going through the motions', in which employee
behaviour is (minimally) congruent with 'realising' the values,
but only in so far as it is calculated that material and/or
symbolic advantage can be gained from managing the appearance of consent. This is very far from being the kind of
internalised commitment displayed by employees in Japanese
firms and in such respected companies as IBM. Even in IBM,
however, the picture has not always been rosy, as Pascale
notes:[15]

> Included in IBM's mechanisms for respecting the indivi-
> dual is a device known as the 'penalty box'. Often a
> person sent to the 'penalty box' has committed a crime
> against the culture – for example, harsh handling of a
> subordinate, overzealousness against the competition,
> gaming the reporting system. The penalty is a move
> sideways which to outsiders looks like a normal assign-
> ment, but insiders know they are off the track.

At the same time, Willmott's position is little more than a
well-argued polemic. Most organisations seeking to present a
coherent and recognisable face to all the world will consider it
quite legitimate to recruit, select, train, motivate, promote and

reward people who will 'fit in' to the organisation's ethical values and strategic goals. The question is not *whether* employees should be socialised, but *how far* the process should go – and this question is, like all others, an issue about ethical values, about whether human beings are means to an end (ie, employed as contributors to the achievement of organisational purposes) or are ends in themselves. As Tony Eccles[16] concedes, 'empowerment' does not mean that employees have complete freedom to do what they like, but rather that (at its best) employees have more authority, resources and latitude to be able to work effectively in the service of the organisation.

Our philosophy is founded on the fact that organisations noted for their strong cultures – Nissan, Marks & Spencer, Sony, Mars – are often noted as well for their superb results and their ability to attract talented people. This is not to say that there is a direct causal relationship between a strong culture and impressive performance, since a strong culture can be dictatorial, complacent, arrogant and intolerant. What matters is the flavour of the culture. The four companies just named, although being 'excellent' organisations, do not recognise themselves as excellent, so they never take their achievements for granted. Such organisations understand that the management of diversity implies the necessity to create co-ordinated teams and unified purposes from the raw material of human resources. This is not the same as the total suppression of individuality. We rest our case on reiterating the opinions of the anonymous Dutchman contributing to a training programme about cultural diversity:

> Sometimes when I hear my company talk about harmonisation, I think they want us all to play the same note. Well, I am a musician, and let me tell you that harmony doesn't mean that; it means that we all play different notes, but together we sound beautiful.[17]

One final point concerns the emphasis placed on the recruitment and selection of 'appropriate' people to work in organisations characterised by strong corporate cultures and powerful core values. The Japanese in particular put great store by working as a group and achieving *wa* – collective harmony and consensus. Within Japanese manufacturing concerns, the unit of production is generally 'the team', a collection of people based on a 'manufacturing cell' within which workers are responsible for actual products rather than a single process. As Delbridge and Turnbull[18] point out:

> It is essential for JIT production that these groups work efficiently and without disruption, and to this end Japanese firms spend considerable time, effort and money on recruitment, induction and 'socialisation', the essence of which is to achieve conformity throughout the workforce. The team itself then takes over in the management of compliance, with the key role assigned to the team leader.

Very typically, the emphasis in recruitment is on *behavioural traits* rather than technical competence, as the personnel director of Komatsu in the UK has made clear:

> Our approach to recruitment has been specific and rigorous. We haven't necessarily taken on the most skilled people, but the ones who have the right attitude to team working and flexibility.[19]

What is so remarkable about this? In our judgement it would be perverse of organisations to recruit people without regard to their attitudes and behavioural inclinations. Nor would doing so be beneficial from the viewpoint of the people recruited, since many of them would soon discover the dissonance between the organisation's priorities and their own personal values.

Values to owners

Owners have two principal rights, at least in principle:

- access to accurate information about the health of the organisation

- receipt of a 'fair' element from the profits generated by the organisation.

Disclosing corporate information to shareholders, for example, ought to be a non-contentious issue. However, managers often fear that if shareholders know too much they will be tempted to interfere too closely, and managerial freedom to act will be reduced. What is worse, shareholders may start to ask awkward questions about managerial remuneration and benefits.

In practice, therefore, disclosure of information to shareholders raises somewhat similar issues to those concerned with disclosure of information to employees. When employees are shareholders, management's inhibitions about the dangers of disclosure are enhanced. As Ogden[20] points out, employers may favour employee (and, by implication, shareholder) involvement, yet fear that if they disclose financial information to their workforce (as they would have to do if embarking on a profit-share process), then employees would demand an increased degree of influence over managerial and strategic decisions.

> Providing information may be time-consuming and costly for management, and slow down decision-making. It may lead to greater militancy and higher wage claims, or produce parity claims between establishments and encourage fragmented bargaining. It may be misinterpreted by trade unions, or used selectively by them. More fundamentally it is feared that disclosure of information may promote challenges and opposition to management's plans and decisions rather than co-operation and support for them. It may . . . reveal conflicts of interest where none were previously perceived.[21]

The idea that involvement and participation will produce superior results to those achieved if the decision-making entity is a single person or small unit evidently does not sit easily with some managers. Indeed, it is clear from several research studies that many executives have a highly partial view about what 'involvement' actually means. A survey of factory managers, for example,[22] found the notion of 'involvement' was viewed in a highly specific and instrumental way. It was not a matter of giving workers 'a say in decisions affecting them', but rather a means whereby 'workers are persuaded to accept the logic that management wishes to follow' and of 'persuading workers to accept "business realities" and to go along with the shop-floor changes that managers saw as necessary.'

Normally, organisations will regard their shareholders simply as one of the groups of stakeholders (whether they like stakeholder theory or not). Shareholders can make a difference. However, their capacity and willingness to do so is limited. Their capacity is restricted by the fact that, usually, shareholders are not a cohesive group and individually lack sufficient power to exert decisive clout – unless they are institutional shareholders. The willingness of shareholders to act is again displayed only rarely, and normally when their resilience has been tested beyond endurance.

Friedman[23] claims such behaviour by shareholders to be deeply unethical. His argument (summarised already in Chapter 2) is that the job of managers is to make as much money as possible for the shareholders. Managers, like other workers, are employees of the owners of the enterprise – the shareholders – and are directly responsible to them. The main aim of shareholders is to maximise their wealth, says Friedman, and managers must pursue that objective exclusively. If managers pursue any additional goals – perhaps in order to satisfy other stakeholders or other values – then their performance will begin to be judged by some non-economic criteria. The use of profits for non-economic purposes will bring profitability down and should in turn depress the share price, thereby making the organisation vulnerable to takeover by less socially-conscious companies or individuals. Thus, argues Friedman, allocating corporate resources to 'social' projects is contrary to the interests of the organisation's owners.

Friedman's argument is simple and straightforward. For that reason alone we find it appealing. However, he misses the point, so far as the 1990s are concerned:

- He ignores the reality of power in organisations. If companies are run by managers then naturally some of them will seek to serve their own interests first, even if in so doing they claim to be acting for the shareholders. They will pursue growth, for example, because of its inherent opportunities for career advancement, self-aggrandisement, and protection against competitive encroachment, despite the fact that growth (especially if it takes the form of mergers and acquisitions) seldom delivers promised profitability or strategic synergy. Of course, we concede that managers may seek growth not primarily for narrow, selfish reasons but simply because they want their organisations to be successful; unfortunately we cannot be certain how far such altruistic loyalty is typical.
- Friedman structures his argument around the proposition that the main aim of shareholders is to maximise their wealth. This itself is a value-judgement and should be tested against reality. In fact, many shareholders are interested in other goals as well as wealth maximisation: they increasingly show concern for the practice of ethical leadership in the organisations where their funds are invested.
- Friedman does not take account of the possibility that the corporate pursuit of some non-economic purposes could actually be good for business and generate more profit rather than less, especially in an age which is less crudely materialistic than the 1960s.

Values towards customers

This book does not set out to teach any lessons in customer care – as a process, as a source of competitive advantage, or as a manifestation of ethical leadership.[24] Nevertheless, a few key points need to be stressed. The phrase 'customer care' is already slightly outmoded and will eventually follow other phrases like 'TQM', 'BPR' and 'empowerment' into the oblivion which waits at the end of the ideas life-cycle. What won't descend into oblivion is the continued need to satisfy customers. This, like the canons of ethical leadership, will go on forever, since customer expectations are not static and competitor innovation is always around.

The idea that all organisations have customers – and that, within organisations, functional departments have customers – is relatively new. Some people have yet to acknowledge that the customer concept applies to them. Some believe that it does, but they would prefer to do nothing, or as little as defensively possible. Some organisations have gone alarmingly wrong in specifying who their 'customers' might be. Some companies are doing their best but are rather better at *talking at* their customers than at *listening to* them. Only a few companies have elevated customers on to the pedestal where, in our view, they rightly belong, and pursue customer-satisfaction and customer-delight with something approaching messianic zeal.

One corporate example will suffice. Rank Xerox has a clear and shared vision, rooted in the customer. Rewards and remuneration reflect a strategic focus on the customer, with pay and bonuses linked to customer-satisfaction measures regularly assessed through direct and indirect surveys. Activities within the company are justified only by the extent to which they can add value for customers, with all employees concentrating on negotiated outputs contributing to customer satisfaction. Strategically, too, IT focuses on the key processes which generate benefits for customers. If customer-satisfaction is the Number One goal, then it can only be achieved by means of the Number Two objective, which is employee-commitment and involvement – especially as the vast majority of customer-interface transactions at 'moments of truth' feature lower-level staff. Rank Xerox have recognised the strength of the argument presented by Susan Newell:[25]

> The issue for firms is . . . to motivate front-line employees to care about the quality of their service or product. The problem is that many organisations try to do this within a framework in which it is very clear to those who are being asked to 'care', that their employers do not care at all for

them. They are asked to do routine, repetitive, dead-end jobs, earning wages often barely above the poverty line; they are expected to obey orders which they have had no involvement in setting and realise that they will be dismissed if it no longer suits the company to keep them on. It is not surprising that in this situation the sales assistant is going to respond with a negative attitude . . . To break this cycle individuals need to be given opportunities to develop their skills and then empowered to put these skills to use.

Rather than empowering workers in such situations, the emphasis is more frequently on increasing control and the reduction of autonomy. Schlesinger and Heskett[26] have found that in situations of low opportunity and power, a destructive cycle is set in motion. Managers argue that there is no point training people who show no commitment, so the decision is made to take even more skill out of the job, which in turn is used as a justification for reducing wages. Computers replace some staff, and monitor those that are left because it is assumed that they cannot be trusted to work without being closely controlled. As Schlesinger and Heskett show, this cycle evokes the kind of performance from sales staff which prompts customers to go elsewhere.

Values towards ourselves (the managers)

Ethical values in themselves are invisible: you cannot directly see them, touch them, feel them. Yet organisations are governed by the shared values of those who have power within the system – and sometimes those values can be traced back to a single person who has chosen like-minded individuals as lieutenants and acolytes. Articulating ethical beliefs – causing them to surface into the conscious corporate mind – can be immensely valuable for a number of reasons:

- They may be challenged against criteria of ethical acceptability and/or their practical consequences in terms of customer retention, employee commitment, and profitability.

- Their operational impact can be assessed. To what extent, for example, is uncritical acceptance of the *status quo* restricting organisational innovation and change?
- They should be examined for internal consistency, since often the ethical framework transmits conflicting messages about, say, the necessity to avoid law-breaking or corner-cutting, yet with the contradictory obligation to meet dead-lines 'no matter what it takes'.
- If the organisation already has a statement of ethical values and a code of conduct, these blueprints need to be matched against employee and customer perceptions of reality, and against a dispassionate self-critical process undertaken by senior executives themselves.

It is very clear that organisations vary in the ethical climates they establish for their members. Not surprisingly, the signals are often confusing. Top management may say one thing, but do another; middle management may exert different pressures. What is important is what top managers **are seen to do**: these words are deliberately emphasised because what top managers are seen to do is much more important than what top management actually does. This can be very unfortunate for the top managers concerned. Their actions may be prompted by adherence to the canons of ethical leadership, yet these same actions can have a very unethical interpretation placed on them by (for example) those on the receiving end, or those indirectly affected, such as employees being made redundant, factories being closed, suppliers being dropped, customers failing to receive compensation. Early, frank, and unambiguous communication can help to undermine the possibility of such misunderstandings, but we are not so sanguine as to believe this will always solve problems.

What top managers are seen to do will establish and reinforce a particular corporate culture. This in turn will determine the way lower-level personnel act and the way the organisation as a whole responds when ethical dilemmas occur. Newcomers soon learn these 'real' values. Newell[27] writes:

> If everybody 'knows' that meeting production deadlines is paramount, then the likelihood of an individual questioning that piece of 'knowledge' is extremely low. Furthermore, it is sustained or reinforced by the systems of rewards and punishments; so it is the unscrupulous production manager who does meet deadlines, regardless of whether this flouts the rules (or even the law), who gets promoted, rather than the manager who misses deadlines because of concern with ensuring that all tests have been done properly.

A classic example of punishment meted out for ethical behaviour, while unethical actions are rewarded, revolves round the Challenger shuttle disaster of 1986.[28] One of the causes of the explosion of the shuttle soon after takeoff was found to have been a problem with the O-ring seal used as part of the attachment between the booster rockets and the shuttle itself. The seal-joining segments were designed and made by the Morton Thiokol Corporation. Two of the Morton Thiokol engineers subsequently testified that they had known about the unreliability of these O-ring seals in very cold weather, and had tried to persuade their senior managers that the planned launch should not proceed. The problem had been taken to a meeting with NASA, but NASA, concerned about funding for future Challenger missions, put pressure on Morton Thiokol to downgrade or even ignore the issue. At a private management meeting within the Morton Thiokol team, the two engineers 'surmised that no one was listening to them, so they gave up'.[29] The company's vice-president for engineering was exhorted to 'take off your engineering hat and put on your management hat'. The Morton Thiokol managers then agreed to recommend launching. The company's actions showed that although safety was theoretically at the top of the ethical agenda, in practice it could be (and was) compromised.

What is especially interesting about the Morton Thiokol case is the fate of the two engineers, Roger Biosjoly and Arnold Thompson, who in effect blew the whistle on their company when testifying to the Presidential Commission enquiry. Both were moved to new jobs and demoted. As we have seen, this is not uncommon treatment for people classified as whistle-blowers. Although it may not be particularly surprising, it nonetheless transmits messages about the likely consequences of ethical action. In accordance with the principles of operant conditioning, we would expect that if unethical behaviour is positively reinforced, through praise and promotion, while ethical behaviour is condemned and leads to demotion, repri-mand, or even dismissal, then many individuals are likely to behave unethically, even though they know their behaviour to be wrong.

One of the elements influencing individuals will be the culture or climate of the organisation, but this influence is not deterministic and has to compete with other influences, some of them deeply embedded in the individual's own ethical constructs. There are no easy answers; if there were, then the debate about ethics would have been resolved centuries ago. We believe, against the background of ethical leadership, that Schermerhorn's seven-step checklist[30] for resolving ethical dilemmas has substantial merit (see Table 9.1).

The crucial part of this process, in ethical terms, is clearly reminding us yet again of the *'Private Eye* Test' outlined in Chapter 2.

We are aware of the dangers of over-simplifying the intract-ability of ethical decision- making, especially in organisations which put short-term profits before moral and social responsi-bilities. In such cases, 'doing the right thing' according to transcendental moral principles may generate damaging or even disastrous consequences for the individual – who, in any event, has to take account of other 'stakeholders'.

On the other hand, for every Morton Thiokol and Chal-lenger O-ring, for every Ford Motor Company and Pinto fuel tank, for every Firestone with its 500-series radial tyre, there

Table 9.1

1 Recognise and clarify the dilemma.
2 Get all the possible facts.
3 List your options – *all of them* (bearing in mind that with all scenarios, there are at least two alternatives).
4 Test each option by asking:
  • Is it legal?
  • Is it right?
  • Is it beneficial?
5 Make your decision.
6 Double-check your decision by asking two more questions:
  • How would I feel if my family found out about this?
  • How would I feel if my decision was printed in the local newspaper?
7 Take action.

are other organisations which genuinely seek to foster a culture of ethical leadership where actions *are* founded on the need to do 'the right thing', regardless of cost. Three examples:

- Johnson & Johnson immediately acted to withdraw one of their drugs from the market-place when there was a slight hint that the product might be contaminated.
- Production-line workers at Nissan and Toyota can press buttons to stop the lines at any time if they detect a problem.
- SmithKline Beecham withdrew all stocks of Lucozade within hours when it was feared that some bottles had been interfered with.

Significance of the 'values domain' model

We have already argued that bringing ethical values to the surface is not only desirable, but is a necessity as part of the effort needed to generate strategic cohesion. Clarifying ethical values as a deliberate exercise has the following outcomes:

The ethical values finally selected for the organisation will have been chosen consciously from a range of alternatives – not merely identified arbitrarily or taken for granted. The act of choosing strengthens commitment.

The ethical values are more likely to be consistent with each other. Values pulling in different directions create role-conflict and cognitive dissonance. People will view inconsistency in the values as an opportunity to ignore them altogether and simply carry on as before.

The ethical values will be few in number. Trying to adopt an excessive number of ethical values will dissipate effort, create confusion, and increase the likelihood of internal inconsistencies.

The ethical values will be actionable. A value which cannot be put into effect becomes a weakness, a hopeless dream, an exercise in pious optimism which fools nobody. Moreover, impossible standards simply present opportunities for the organisation to view itself as deficient.

The ethical values will be performance-enhancing. Properly designed ethical values are an enabling device – a means of shaping actions, initiatives and behaviour so that people can contribute more positively to performance objectives.

The ethical values will be attractive and aspirational. People need to be uplifted by the articulation of ethical values with which they can identify without their own consciences being imperilled.

The ethical values can be communicated. If they are complicated, or cannot be expressed in everyday language, then some will ignore them, some will misunderstand, and some will resent what they perceive to be patronising treatment.

Summary

A large proportion of this chapter has concentrated on the benefits to be gained from clarifying the values conventionally associated with ethical leadership. These values, once discussed, debated, accepted or modified, can become the ethical framework for the organisation's strategic direction.

In addition we have shown the essential links between ethics, vision, values and strategy. Such links are indispensable not only from a strategic viewpoint but also at the operational level, if managers, professionals and employees are to perceive ethical leadership as a significant opportunity for ethical advantage and a legitimate constraint against unethical action.

In the next and final chapter, we review the critical elements for success in promoting ethical leadership as a way of corporate and managerial life.

References

1. John Gill and Sue Whittle, 'Management by panacea: accounting for transience', *Journal of Management Studies*, Vol. 30, No. 2, March 1993, pp. 281–296.
2. Pepi Sappal, 'Consultant rewrites rulebook to incorporate ethical agenda', *Consult*, May/June 1995, pp. 12–13.
3. A. Hodgson, 'Deming's never-ending road to quality', *Personnel Management*, July 1987, pp. 40–44.
4. John Gill and Sue Whittle, *op. cit.*, p. 290.
5. Torsten H. Nilson, *Chaos Marketing – How to Win in a Turbulent World*, Maidenhead, McGraw-Hill, 1995, p. 85.
6. John Humble, *Corporate Values – The bottom line corporation*, Reading, Digital Equipment Company, 1992.
7. Dave Francis, *Step-by-Step Competitive Strategy*, London, Routledge, 1994, pp. 103–114.
8. Dave Francis, *op. cit.*, p. 106.
9. See David Brown, 'There's no money in it', *Daily Telegraph*, 16 May 1995, p. 20.
10. Toru Nishikawa, 'New product planning at Hitachi', *Journal of Long Range Planning*, Vol. 22, No. 4, 1989, pp. 20–24.

11. Dave Francis, *op. cit.*, p. 107.
12. Hugh Willmott, 'Strength is ignorance; slavery is freedom: managing culture in modern organisations', *Journal of Management Studies*, Vol. 30, No. 4, July 1993, pp. 515–552. The phrase 'sacred canopy' is taken from P. Berger, *The Social Reality of Religion*, Harmondsworth, Penguin Books, 1973.
13. Hugh Willmott, *op. cit.*, p. 534.
14. The phrase 'our people are our greatest asset' is now a cliché which deserves to be buried with full military honours. At the European Association of Personnel Management's 1995 conference (reported in *People Management*, 13 July 1995, p. 19), Professor Paul Evans of INSEAD claimed that 'People are often a company's greatest liability too. It's not people, but skills, that are most important.'
15. Richard Pascale, 'The paradox of "corporate culture": reconciling ourselves to socialisation', *California Management Review*, Vol. 27, No. 2, 1985, pp. 26–41.
16. Tony Eccles, *Succeeding with Change – Implementing Action-driven Strategies*, Maidenhead, McGraw-Hill, 1994, p. 185.
17. Cited in Kevan Hall, 'Worldwide vision in the workplace', *People Management*, 18 May 1995, pp. 20–25.
18. Rick Delbridge and Peter Turnbull, 'Human resource maximisation: the management of labour under just-in-time manufacturing systems', in Paul Blyton and Peter Turnbull, (eds), *Reassessing Human Resource Management*, London, Sage, 1992, pp. 56–73.
19. Quoted in A. Gabb, 'Komatsu makes the earth move', *Management Today*, November 1989, pp. 77–81.
20. Stuart Ogden, 'The limits to employee involvement: profit sharing and disclosure of information', *Journal of Management Studies*, Vol. 29, No. 2, March 1992, pp. 229–248.
21. Stuart Ogden, *op. cit.*, p. 239.
22. P. Edwards, 'Factory managers: their role in personnel management and their place in the company', *Journal of Management Studies*, Vol. 24, No. 5, September 1987, pp. 479–501.
23. Milton Friedman, *Capitalism and Freedom*, Chicago, University of Chicago Press, 1962.
24. For more information on the complex business of satisfying customers see Ted Johns, *Perfect Customer Care*, London, Arrow, 1994.
25. Susan Newell, *The Healthy Organisation – Fairness, ethics and effective management*, London, Routledge, 1995, p. 3.
26. L. Schlesinger and J. Heskett, 'The service-driven service com-

pany', *Harvard Business Review*, September–October 1991, pp. 71–81.

27. Susan Newell, *op. cit.*, p. 185.
28. See William H. Starbuck and Frances J. Milliken, 'Challenger: fine-tuning the odds until something breaks', *Journal of Management Studies*, Vol. 25, No. 4, July 1988, pp. 319–340.
29. William H. Starbuck and Frances J. Milliken, *op. cit.*, p. 332.
30. J. R. Schermerhorn, *Management for Productivity*, New York, John Wiley, 1989, p. 233.

10

♟ Conclusions: Critical Success Factors for Ethical Leadership

Introduction

Achieving a competitive advantage founded on ethical leadership is just about as problematic as achieving any other cultural change. It is time-consuming, costly (if taken seriously), uncomfortable (especially for those whose tried and tested beliefs are being challenged) and, in the short term, unrewarding.

Yet the long-term benefits are potentially huge. Inaction and apathy are even more unattractive than the pain of grasping the nettle. In Chapter 2 we explored the growing concerns about the way in which organisations behave in relation to their own people, the ways in which they allocate resources, their occasionally cavalier attitudes towards customers, the damage they can do to their surroundings, and the legacies they leave others to clear up. Faced with these concerns, there are two types of solution.

The first is to increase governmental regulation. This option is not cost-effective and does not work. As the Inland Revenue has already found, legislation cannot prevent unethical individuals from assiduously seeking out potential loopholes. Further, a legislative or regulatory approach is almost invariably proscriptive. Focusing on what is forbidden encourages a satisfiying approach to ethical behaviour in which minimal levels of compliance criteria become maximum standards of performance.

Much to be preferred is our second solution, namely, self-regulation within organisations themselves, either individually or collectively. Even self-regulation, we concede, may produce nothing more than an illusory feeling in the ethical comfort-zone, especially if 'self-regulation' is simply PR-speak for 'defensive marketing' aimed at the continued preservation of existing 'freedoms'. Properly conceived, however, self-regulation can generate a corporate culture in which it would be unthinkable for employees to behave unethically.

This is not a pipe-dream. We have already named some organisations whose ethical criteria – and everyday behaviour – are beyond reproach. What they have done, and what they do to maintain their ethical leadership, can be emulated or, better still, exceeded.

In this concluding chapter, we discuss the issues – 14 of them – which we believe have to be addressed before moves towards ethical leadership can be viewed as successful. Virtually all the issues have been pursued elsewhere in our book: here they are reinforced.

The 14 critical success factors

1 There has to be a clear, cogent link between the ethical values and ethical leadership on the one hand, and the vision and strategic direction on the other.   In Chapter 9 we established that organisations are only effective when the differing dimensions of the 'values domain' are brought into positive alignment. Equally, the McKinsey 7S model[1] is based on the necessity for the elements to fit together, so that the 'strategy' coincides with the 'shared values.' However, the 7S model highlights the importance of three relationships which are vital to a deeper understanding of the nature of corporate management, and which are equally vital to the success of an ethical leadership programme.

First, the 7S model does not recognise the significance of the connection between the private values of employees and the shared (ethical) values of the organisation. Through the concept of Staff the 7S model acknowledges the need to have people who fit well with the other S's, but McKinsey only sees the control and behaviour benefits for the organisation. For this reason, the fulfilment and feelings of worth – which 'shared values' can ignite in employees – are unintentionally ignored.

Table 10.1

The McKinsey 7S Framework

Hard S's
- Structure
- Systems
- Strategy

Soft S's
- Shared values
- Staff
- Skills
- Style

Source: R. Pascale and A. Athos, *The Art of Japanese Management*, London, Penguin Books, 1982, p. 202.

Recruits joining an organisation are not blank slates on whom appropriate messages can be inscribed: our discussion of alternative ethical principles in Chapter 3 showed that they bring an emotional and affective baggage whose contents are just as legitimate a subject of potential employer interest as, say, the possession of technical and occupational skills.

Another difficulty with the 7S framework is that it does not emphasise the importance of behaviour standards. Yet by creating some behaviour standards that capture the essence of both the strategic direction and the moral logic in the organisation, top management can ensure that the 'shared values' fit the 'strategy'. The behaviour standards then become the means by which this fit is accomplished. Unfortunately, the 7S model has no such powerful integrating thought. It relies on a loose concept of 'fit' that encourages managers simplistically to eliminate incongruent elements from the organisation. We find this approach less satisfactory – indeed, less ethical – than an approach which emphasises positive behaviour standards as a goal to be attained. Such standards are reflected in corporate imperatives like 'Putting People First' (British Airways) and 'Management By Wandering Around' (Hewlett-Packard).

Thirdly, the 7S framework gives little attention to vision. In

Chapter 3 and elsewhere, we have stressed the necessity for vision and ethical values to be made explicit. We believe their relevance and potential impact are so impressive that they should be separately codified.

Pascale and Athos comment tellingly[2] on the foolishness of believing that organisational change is simply a matter of targeting one or two elements in the 7S framework.

> Many executives are unwilling to work at some of the S's, or are so impatient they cannot sustain the effort for long, so they focus on those they can change by fiat – notably Strategy and Structure, and, of course, Systems . . . . If attention to the other S's is intermittent, faddish, and if it is liable to cancellation at the first signal of reduced profits, the chances are good that your company is in . . . trouble.

2 Systematic reward/punishment and communication procedures must regularly reinforce and promote the principles of ethical leadership. Mechanisms for encouraging commitment include

- managerial involvement and role-modelling from the top down.
- recruitment and selection practices which adhere to ethical leadership principles in themselves but which also seek out individuals who are likely to be receptive to the behaviour standards involved. Remember that the intention is not to produce a company of clones, but an organisation of morally mature, autonomously-reasoning people whose actions are consistent with the organisation's ethical posture.
- education, training and development programmes which, again, live by the criteria of ethical leadership and which promote induction training and all performance-improvement activities geared towards management, sales, customer-relations, and the acquisition of 'people skills'.
- communication systems designed to enlighten and motivate employees on a continuing basis – hence the need for the

concepts of ethical leadership to be revamped at frequent intervals to prevent communication overkill.

- ethical leadership awareness constantly reinforced through corporate publications (annual reports, PR documents, employee reports, customer literature, and so forth), management meetings, and conference contributions.
- team briefings/meetings containing regular slots for progress reports.
- recognition and reward processes which acknowledge conduct that displays exemplary adherence to the ethical values. The recognition processes in particular should involve senior and top-level people (with personal presentations, ceremonies or communications), and to achieve maximum impact should be very high-profile in order to spread the word widely.
- ombudsman or other systems to act as a conduit for employee queries and the reporting of ethical leadership violations, in preference to external whistle-blowing.
- attention to high-risk roles (eg procurement) in terms of the special dangers involved.
- periodic certification and auditing to ensure continued compliance with the ethical values and code of conduct. Auditing mechanisms should tackle not only explicit measurement criteria, but also the implicit behaviour codes, or the way people behave when they think nobody is watching. This kind of monitoring is much harder to carry out, but has to be attempted if auditing is to be meaningful. The use of anonymous attitude surveys is one approach. If such surveys yield unpleasant data, then at least management has a basis on which to take action, however unwelcome.
- enforcement procedures and sanctions which are well-defined, explicit, and fair. Preferably, adherence to the canons of ethical leadership is specified as an essential condition of employment – which is yet another way of making it clear that the company means business.

3 Visible support and role-modelling from the company's top managers and especially from the chairman/CEO. Yet again we have to say that it is not enough for senior executives simply to mouth the words. As Ferdinand de Bakker[3] puts it:

> The problem with some value statements is that employees read them and then look around. And it is here where most mission statement programmes are being killed. This is because management is judged constantly and its behaviour is benchmarked all the time against the values. Often there's no visible change in the behaviour of top management and so employees are encouraged to do the same.

So senior personnel need to take part actively in ethics monitoring and business-conduct evaluation meetings. They need to raise ethical leadership issues at appraisal sessions with their own staff. All expressions of cynicism and self-doubt must be stilled. It takes only one throw-away, facetious remark from one individual to undo the positive impact of 100 supportive signals from the top team as a whole.

4 Incorporation of ethical leadership principles into performance appraisal and PRP systems. In Chapter 8 we argued that desired behaviour is much more likely to take place if individuals believe that their appraisals, their rewards and their careers are likely to be affected.

Norwich Union is one company which has explicitly linked its ethical values and code of conduct to performance review. Rank-Xerox, whose supreme dedication to customers is well known, reserves up to 30 per cent of the remuneration of senior executives to achievement of performance goals derived from customer feedback.

5 The broad sweep of ethical leadership needs to be translated into ambitious yet achievable targets. What is rewarded, gets done. What is rewarded, needs to be measured. Without measurement there is room for subjectivity, and subjective judgements breed dissent. We do not subscribe to the crude belief that the only things which matter are the things which are measurable, but at the same time we do argue that if ethical leadership is to become a reality, it has to be quantified, albeit indirectly, through performance measures from which progress can be inferred.

Many corporate ethical values lend themselves readily enough to the creation of quantifiable, time-bounded targets. Here are a few examples:

- Values towards customers – capable of being measured by
  - market research surveys
  - qualitative techniques (focus groups)
  - complaint analysis
  - comparison with customer-service standards delivered by benchmark competitors and other organisations.
- Values towards people – capable of being measured by
  - in-house attitude/communication surveys
  - hotline facilities take-up levels
  - workforce retention/absenteeism/sickness statistics
  - specification and achievement of 'bold goal' performance-improvement targets for individuals and teams.
- Values towards the environment – capable of being measured by
  - proportion of corporate resources made available for social and environmental projects
  - accident/health statistics among employees
  - public perception studies and media exposure analysis.

For individual employees, the specification of at least one performance-improvement objective linked to ethical leadership is appropriate in the appraisal system.

6 In the process of operationalising the principles of ethical leadership, indicator and contra-indicator behaviour standards and norms need to be generated. Ethical values have to be supplemented by a specification of the behaviours considered appropriate and those viewed as unacceptable, so that nobody need be in any doubt about what ethical leadership means for them. Such behaviour standards can be used as part of the input to performance review. They are not unlike the criteria used when defining competency levels at various grades in the organisation.

7 To promote the behavioural skills needed for ethical leadership, training and education resources must be mobilised – but cost-effectively. We said in Chapter 7 that training linked to the ethical values will be more effective if facilitated by line managers working with in-house training specialists or external consultants. Involvement by the organisation's line managers helps to reinforce beliefs about the significance of the ethical leadership initiative and, as a significant by-product, compels these managers to familiarise themselves more thoroughly with the values and their implications. The contribution of external consultants is especially valuable in coaching line managers up to acceptable levels of competence in workshop-leading skills, but also in helping to avoid incestuous and complacent attitudes within the training itself.

8 The approaches to implementing ethical leadership and monitoring ethical values compliance should be structured, open and fair. A principal benefit from installing a well-defined implementation process is that it is easier to understand and apply than unexpressed, informal and arbitrary procedures. The more explicit the system, moreover, the greater is the likelihood that it will command allegiance, especially if it relies upon the co-operative efforts of a multi-function monitoring team from, say, HR, corporate administration, auditing, and legal departments. For smaller organisations, HR is the natural repository for ethical leadership implementation and monitoring, though more commonly as a monitor of last resort rather than as a first court of appeal.

9 It is preferable to generate a dual-element compliance system, using both trust and monitoring together. Excessive concentration purely on compliance and enforcement (negative words in themselves), plus punishment for deviant behaviour, will send out misleading signals:

- The criteria for ethical leadership, intended to be viewed as the minimum standards for acceptable behaviour, will become the maximum standards as well, as individuals comply with the basic requirements *but no more*. Conformity with the ethical values and associated code will be purely instrumental, based on fear of the consequences of non-compliance (if discovered).
- Individuals will work hard to find ways of circumventing the expectations associated with ethical leadership, while appearing to satisfy them. As experience with compliance in the world of financial services has shown, human ingenuity (sometimes supplemented by corporate guile) is limitless when confronted by the challenge of by-passing control systems, so any attempt to create comprehensive compliance systems is doomed.
- People in the organisation will believe, rightly or wrongly, that ethical leadership is only being pursued for defensive reasons which have nothing to do with any ideological or moral conviction.

By contrast, if compliance becomes internalised, then implementation of ethical values can rely more on imperatives like mutual respect and trust. This likelihood is increased if, over time, the organisation develops some cultural homogeneity in ethical behaviour through its recruitment, selection, training, reward, and career progression practices.

Nevertheless, we live in the real world. The real world has some naughty, wicked or misguided people in it. Some of them are working in organisations, subverting the company from inside. Formal monitoring and surveillance is essential if only as a deterrent; good intentions and wishful thinking are insufficient mechanisms for ensuring that leadership becomes ethical rather than manipulative.

Annual or periodic certification, as a re-affirmation of ethical values acceptance, is particularly useful in order to remind people about their commitments, both positive and negative, and the possible dangers of contravention and concealment. Several organisations use certification in one form or another; one possible framework from an anonymous company cited by Manley[4] is given in Table 10.2.

Table 10.2

I have received and read the Company Code of Conduct.
I certify that I am presently in full compliance with the policies stated in the Code of Conduct, and that I have no direct knowledge or factual evidence of any present violation of them by another employee, except as I have specifically disclosed to the Company.
Signature: _____
Name: (print) _____
Department or Group: _____
Location: _____ Date: _____

10 All parts of the organisation must be involved in the implementation of ethical leadership. This is especially important if the organisation wants to avoid creating the impression that ethical leadership is just another top management 'flavour-of-the-month'. If the ethical values and ethical leadership principles are transmitted to every sector of the organisation, with proper attention to the difficulties of implementation at the 'coal-face', then this says something about the significance of the exercise and also transmits powerful messages about the significance of the groups to which the ethical values are addressed.

11 Employee endorsement of ethical leadership will be reinforced if there is a multi-faceted approach to implementation. Establishing many points of leverage, and using a multiplex approach to influence and persuasion, will be key factors in successful adoption of ethical leadership ideals; business conduct committees, hotlines, ombudsmen, and resources to answer employee questions, are prime examples. Building ethical values criteria into performance-appraisal systems, specifying continuous-improvement targets linked to the ethical values, publicising progress and achievements, are others.

Maximising use of in-house communications media is equally vital. Top management can take opportunities to link their regular communications into the ethical values, and therefore demonstrate continuing commitment to the issue. All functions should integrate the ethical values into their documents and software so that, for example, they are printed in company diaries and as part of purchasing contracts.

Positive measures for continual communication of the ethical values can include:

- awareness workshops for all employees
- clear-cut requirements for the ideals of ethical leadership to be communicated to all new employees (as part of selection, induction, and contracts of employment)
- an obligation for all line managers to review periodically (perhaps within the appraisal process) every employee's understanding of the ethical values and of what ethical leadership means for them
- articles and features about ethical leadership in corporate newspapers – with an opportunity for queries to be published and discussed in print, case-studies analysed, and ideas for further development (possibly inspired by other organisations) being canvassed
- posters about ethical leadership and the ethical values displayed in conspicuous places
- an ethical-values agenda item at team meetings
- dissemination of the ethical values in all employee publications
- circulation of anecdotal and statistical information about

calls to the corporate hotline, or scenarios investigated by the ombudsman
- building the ethical values into all PCs and network systems
- reiteration of the ethical values on restaurant menu-cards and many other standard in-house documents where space is currently under-utilised.

If all this looks like communication overkill, we should make it clear that we are not suggesting blanket coverage using all the mechanisms listed above at the same time. As with all communications, it is essential to ring the changes – not only in the selection of media, but in the way the message is designed and in the target audiences towards whom specific messages are directed. The marketing department should know all about ways of generating interest in new products, sustaining interest at the peak of the life-cycle, and reviving interest in a flagging concept. It is a source of constant surprise to us that internal corporate communicators talk to their marketing colleagues as infrequently as they do.

12 Implementation is more effective if employees are encouraged to report improper, illegal or unethical activities.   As already noted, many organisations provide hot-lines or other mechanisms which allow employees to disclose concerns about the behaviour of others. These procedures operate as safety-valves. They reduce the likelihood of, and pretext for, whistle-blowing to external media sources.

13 The ethical values and the code of conduct – ethical leadership in action – need to be revised from time to time in order to keep them alive and up-to-date.   The ethical values of today are unlikely to be directly relevant to the needs of the organisation five years from now. Ethical leadership will remain as relevant as it is now, but what it means in terms of behaviour will inevitably change. Just as 'customer satisfaction' is a movable feast, so behaviour standards or conduct codes must always reflect the aspirations of the moment. Attitude surveys and interviews can measure developments in employee, customer, supplier, and other stakeholder perceptions – their results can be used as guidelines for companies that want to keep pace.

For organisations which see ethical leadership as an opportunity for competitive advantage, however, reacting to surveys will not be enough. Proactive leadership requires flair, imagination, conviction, creativity, and the willingness to take risks – to anticipate the ethical requirements of the marketplace and even to shape those emerging requirements through ethical leadership itself. In the field of ethics, being a leader is preferable to being a follower. Merely pursuing and copying the principles pioneered by others raises legitimate suspicions about commitment.

14 It has to be recognised that ethical leadership does not mean shelving hard and unpleasant decisions. Faced with tough decisions, managers can put off making them, and may be even more inclined to procrastinate, if they fear that selecting unpleasant options will jeopardise their perceived adherence to the ethical values. The dilemma is particularly conspicuous when the need for competitive efficiency, or a business downturn, call for headcount reductions. To put off the evil day, argues Sir Adrian Cadbury,[5] is unethical in itself because, almost inevitably, it will result in more serious and more widespread adverse consequences later.

Commitment to ethical leadership, moreover, still requires organisations to operate commercially. Cadbury describes how his grandfather had been commissioned by Queen Victoria in 1900 to provide bars of chocolate for soldiers serving in South Africa. Deeply opposed to the Boer War, but intent on building a successful business, grandfather Cadbury resolved the issue by accepting the order, but carrying it out at cost. Using examples like this, Cadbury argues that simplistic ethical 'signposts', glibly presented by single-minded commentators, do not offer satisfactory counsel – not only for ethically complex scenarios within the organisation, but also for business transactions across cultural frontiers.

In doing business with China, for instance, it is the 'Chinese way' to accept, indeed to expect, 'hospitality' as a way of strengthening relationships and creating a social credit upon which one may draw in the future. Business deals are often complemented with a gift, and those who stick out against such practices on grounds of 'principle' can suffer commercially for what is seen as a gratuitous defiance of convention. The problem in the Chinese world, of course, as it is elsewhere, is to determine the point at which 'convention' turns into corruption.

Conclusion: reprise

We are conscious that some of what we have said is formidable – in terms of the challenges posed by defining precisely what 'ethical leadership' signifies, by implementing it, and by sustaining the ethical values linked to ethical leadership. Part of our material is also ambiguous and imprecise. We make no apology for this. The issues surrounding 'ethics' are always ambiguous, multi-faceted, potentially confusing. As we have said before, if ethical problems could be resolved easily, they would not require sustained attention for thousands of years. Of course, for single-issue interest groups (like those opposed to the export of live animals), ethical problems *are* easily resolved. Because the members of such groups are single-minded, they take no account of the interests of other parties (or stakeholders), and they can then display what has been described as 'the ethical superiority of the uninvolved'.

In the real world, and in particular the world of organisations, life is not so simple. Organisations *are* involved: they understand that adopting (or changing) an ethical posture is going to have implications for the business, and conceivably for competitive survival. It is tempting to do nothing, to carry on as before, especially as there can be no certainty that confronting the issues of ethical leadership will prove profitable. The temptation to do nothing is reinforced when one contemplates the effort required.

Our position is that *doing nothing is the most dangerous thing the organisation can do*. Doing nothing implies a willingness to stand still while everything else moves on. Doing nothing suggests complacency, inertia and smug self-satisfaction – dangerous in a competitive environment. So let us once again rehearse the six main reasons why it has to be in the long-term interest of the organisation and its managers to foster a culture of ethical leadership.

Ethical leadership is good for business. Increasingly, sophisticated customers and shareholders expect organisations to behave ethically and will be prepared to favour organisations which make convincing and credible claims about their ethical stance.

Ethical leadership makes the organisation's own employees feel good. It seems plausible to suppose that morale and psychological well-being are likely to be high in organisations which have a reputation for ethical behaviour. Further, such organisations will attract employees with similar aspirations.

Ethical leadership has a self-interested component so far as the organisation's top managers are concerned. In recent years there has been a dramatic growth in instances of criminal charges being taken out against individual executives and directors, as well as against corporate entities. On occasion senior managers can be held accountable for the acts of their employees, even though they had no knowledge about what was going on. The corporate-wide implementation of principles linked to ethical leadership should reduce the likelihood of such eventualities by encouraging employees to act ethically (rather than taking the short cuts which led to the *Herald of Free Enterprise* disaster).

Ethical leadership enables organisations to control and influence their own destinies. If organisations create and sustain their own ethically-acceptable standards, then the pressure to increase legal regulation is reduced. This ultimately, and in turn, reduces costs, because regulation is expensive, limits freedom in decision-making, and constrains corporate power in favour of government power.

Ethical leadership reflects increasing acceptance of Argenti's 'no harm' and 'engagement' principles. More and more people reject the premise that shareholders' rights are all-important. They argue instead for the adoption of a model targeted towards 'beneficiaries', but incorporating elements of stakeholder theory in the sense that the manager's job is to find a balance between the interests of all those who have a 'stake' in the organisation.

Ethical leadership coincides with society's expectations about how organisations should conduct themselves. The argument here is simple: society expects organisations to assume social responsibilities; because organisations operate under franchises from society – in effect, organisations are sanctioned by society to achieve objectives beneficial to society – then they must meet those expectations. If they do not, society will remove the franchise by not buying the products or services on offer, by not coming forward as employees, or, ultimately, by implementing legally-enforceable prohibitions.

In this book we have argued the case for ethical leadership as strongly as we can. We have shown the importance of the issue, demonstrated its unavoidable complexities, and discussed the benefits for organisations. In many instances we have cited practical examples to show what organisations are *saying* about ethical leadership and, even more important, what they are *doing* about it. Where these organisations have led, there is plenty of opportunity to follow – and, by doing better, to reap the rewards.

References

1. Richard Pascale and Anthony Athos, *The Art of Japanese Management*, London, Penguin Books, 1982, p. 202.
2. Richard Pascale and Anthony Athos, *op. cit.*, pp. 203–204.
3. Ferdinand de Bakker, 'The elements of a mission statement' in Timothy R.V. Foster, *101 Great Mission Statements: How the World's Leading Companies Run Their Businesses*, London, Kogan Page, 1992, p. 30.
4. Walter W. Manley II, *The Handbook of Good Business Practice*, London, Routledge, 1992, p. 262.
5. Sir Adrian Cadbury, 'Ethical managers make their own rules', *Harvard Business Review*, September–October 1987, pp. 69–73.

 **Index**